DARE TO BE

ADVANCE PRAISE FOR THE BOOK

'One of the entrepreneurs featured in *Dare to Be* says that we are so defined by other people's idea of success that our inner voice gets drowned. This is so true in a woman's context in India, as the rule books, expected patterns of behaviour and aspirations are most often set by others. So it is heartening to read in this book from Rinku Paul and Puja Singhal the refreshing stories of women entrepreneurs who defy tradition, who, having found "success" in the conventional sense, finally decide to listen to their inner voices. In doing so, they find alternate routes to fulfilment and change their lives for the better. In the unending efforts to retrieve their forgotten and neglected selves, many times, women find inner constraints more daunting than external circumstances. Eventually, it is a battle against our inner scripts that dictate the limits of what we can be. This book offers some inspiring examples of people who could rewrite their scripts and come through.'

Anu Aga, director, Thermax Limited

'*Dare to Be* by Rinku Paul and Puja Singhal is more than just an anthology of high-achieving women. It is indeed inspirational, for these daring journeys, as the authors suggest, were never meant to turn out the way they did. For instance, who'd imagine a career from copy-writing to comedy or capturing hearts and minds through soulful Sufi music. For me, personally, the book is deeply evocative of all that we can do if we put our hearts and minds to it: as also opening out a wonderful world where the *can* is more operative than *will*. To that end, the authors have strung together some fine tales of success written in an easy manner, which almost makes you a fellow traveller on these incredible journeys that have been essayed.'

Suhel Seth, author, columnist

'[This is] a carefully selected group of women, united by their passion to dream and do big, beautifully put together. I have always believed the future belongs to women, and the women in this book show why.'

Aroon Purie, chairman and editor-in-chief, India Today Group

DARE TO BE

14 FEARLESS WOMEN
WHO GAVE WINGS TO THEIR DREAMS

RINKU PAUL
PUJA SINGHAL

EBURY PRESS
An imprint of Penguin Random House

EBURY PRESS

USA | Canada | UK | Ireland | Australia
New Zealand | India | South Africa | China | Singapore

Ebury Press is part of the Penguin Random House group of companies whose addresses can be found at global.penguinrandomhouse.com

Published by Penguin Random House India Pvt. Ltd
4th Floor, Capital Tower 1, MG Road,
Gurugram 122 002, Haryana, India

Penguin
Random House
India

First published by Penguin Books India 2016

10 9 8 7 6 5 4

The views and opinions expressed in this book are the authors' own and the facts are as reported by them which have been verified to the extent possible, and the publishers are not in any way liable for the same.

ISBN 9788184007565

Typeset in Adobe Garamond Pro by Manipal Digital Systems, Manipal

Printed at Repro India Limited

www.penguin.co.in

FSC
www.fsc.org
MIX
Paper from responsible sources
FSC® C047271

This is a legitimate digitally printed version of the book and therefore might not have certain extra finishing on the cover.

To my dad
Miss you more than words can ever say

Rinku

To my kids
Keep the dreamer in you alive

Puja

CONTENTS

INTRODUCTION

A decade and a half into the corporate rat race, diligently climbing up the ladder and living by the monthly pay cheque, when we finally mustered up the courage to take the entrepreneurial leap, little did we know then that our own journey would lead us towards chronicling those of many others.

Having stumbled and fallen several times, plagued by self-doubt and naysayers, what we longed for more than anything else those days were fellow travellers on this difficult but hugely fulfilling path. In an ecosystem where generations have grown up ruing the lack of professional female role models, we are fortunate to have crossed paths with some amazing female entrepreneurs. Their stories are all the more inspiring as they have not only 'dared' to undertake seismic career shifts in following their calling, but have also actively taken up the role of mentoring other women harbouring entrepreneurial ambitions.

That was when the germ of this book was sown. We wanted to infuse the women's entrepreneurial and creative ecosystem with meaningful storytelling—tales that our fellow travellers can draw inspiration from.

Given the fact that India ranks a low 70 among 77 countries covered in the 2015 female entrepreneurship index brought out by the Washington-based Global Entrepreneurship and Development Institute, which measures the 'health of the entrepreneurship eco-systems', the stories are even more precious.

The book tells the tale of fourteen women who have overcome numerous hurdles to carve paths of their own, giving up conventional well-paying jobs in the process. Chosen from across the professional spectrum, these women are inspirational in that they have not only managed to get past issues such as financial limitations, fears and vulnerabilities, but have also held their ground against naysayers, a patriarchal set-up, the proverbial glass ceiling and more.

In two accounts in particular, is also hidden the tale of several women who had to contend with mid-career breaks following motherhood. These women, however, had the resilience to turn their callings into their careers the second time around, and very successfully so.

The women featured include:

- founders of successful commercial start-ups, as well as those whose businesses are driven by a social purpose, and
- bloggers, musicians, dancers, stand-up comedians, authors, motivational speakers and coaches who chose passion over money to eventually attain both creative satisfaction and commercial success.

All the stories have a few common themes that will resonate with women who have either taken the road to entrepreneurship and self-employment or are sitting on the fence, held back by myriad fears. Below in no particular order are some of the beliefs expressed by these women that became the underlying themes for the book.

- *'If being an entrepreneur is tough, then being a woman entrepreneur is tougher, and being a young woman entrepreneur is tougher still'*—There is no denying the fact that these women made their mark in a male-dominated environment where glass ceilings are a reality. Probe them and they have many stories to tell where they were written off professionally solely on account of their gender. Having said that, none of them were cowed, choosing instead to stand tall and prove their mettle.
- *'You cannot align your chips'*—None of these women had considered entrepreneurship as a career choice to begin with. In fact, some of them had even sworn off entrepreneurship early in their lives. Yet, when their calling beckoned, they gave it all their heart. They speak from experience when they say that there is never a perfect time to take the leap. Most of them took the leap after spending many resilient years climbing the corporate ladder.
- *'When you have to choose between passion and money, choose passion, and money will eventually follow'*—Many of the women entrepreneurs featured in the book had to face a tough choice between following their passion and the stability of a steady salary; to add to their woes, most of them were part of the EMI economy. All of them chose to follow their passion and ended up never regretting their decision. What they learnt along their journey was that if you give something your all, money eventually follows.

- *'As long as you are sure of a roof over your head and food on your table, you cannot go too wrong'*—The one thing that all of them unanimously agree on is the need to have a support mechanism in place, should things not work out well. Imagining the worst-case scenario helped dispel undue fears that otherwise threatened to paralyse decision-making. Having said that, the plan was to work like there was no Plan B.
- *'Rejection means nothing more than someone not being able to see what you see'*—It is a testimony to their spirit that they never looked at rejection as anything more than a temporary setback, convinced that each rejection only brought them that much closer to their goal. While many of them took a number of detours along their journey, what they are convinced about is the fact that even if you do not achieve what you initially set out to do, you learn much more about yourself than you would have by staying in your comfort zone.
- *'People who have a voice need to give back to society'*—What also unites all of them is the fact that, if anything, success has made them humble. Driven by a desire to contribute to the success of other women, many of them have even institutionalized their efforts to give back what they have received in abundant measure. Sairee Chahal and Sheroes.in are working to create a career community for women, offering them access to career resources, information and community sharing.
- *'It is better to live with "Oh, shit!" than with "What if?"'*—A compelling sentiment voiced by most of the women in this book is that when life draws to a close, they would prefer to be able to count their regrets on

their fingers instead of living in the shadow of what could have happened had they pursued their passions.

Amidst all these life lessons, a note of caution on what the book does not intend to do.

The book isn't intended to be either a sociological treatise on the times, or a business case study. It is but a chronicle of life, one that documents the journeys of women who have had the courage to choose paths that were less trodden, albeit immensely satisfying.

What the book also does not intend to do is to become an irresponsible call to dump corporate careers in favour of following one's heart. In fact, woman after woman has sounded the note of caution to conduct your own 'litmus test'. What the book is, though, is an impassioned appeal to be true to oneself and let that guide one's life and career path.

As co-authors, both of us have lived and breathed this book for many months. While the ever present 'I' in the narrative is either of us, it could well be the voice of every woman who is keen to give wings to her dreams and hence is probing these fearless stories. Should these stories force any one of you to dust yourself off after a fall and keep going, we would have achieved what we set out to do.

NEETI PALTA

Stand-up comedian

Founder:	Loony Goons
Past Corporate Avatar:	Senior creative director, J. Walter Thomson; head writer, Miditech
Education:	Alumna of Symbiosis Institute of Media and Communication
Honours and Awards:	Devi Award, 2014; Best Stand-up Comic Award at the Oz Fest
Just when you thought you had heard it all:	Scriptwriter for the Bollywood film, *O Teri*

HAVING THE LAST LAUGH

As senior creative director at J. Walter Thomson (JWT)—India's largest advertising agency—Neeti Palta had everything going for her. Till she gave it all up to become the voice of the muppets for the immensely popular children's TV show, Gali Gali Sim Sim. *She then took an even bolder step as she ventured into the nascent and male-dominated field of stand-up comedy, much to her family's consternation. The only thing that kept her going was her passionate belief in her craft. Today, she is highly regarded as one of the very few female stand-up comedians in India, and has her calendar filled with events and gigs all over the country and the world. This is her story.*

'98 per cent of all comedians feel obliged to be funny when interviewed. Less than 2 per cent succeed'—Mokokoma Mokhonoana, philosopher, social critic

Just as Neeti and I settle into a busy coffee shop in plush Select Citywalk in New Delhi for our meeting, a middle-aged man strides up to us purposefully. 'Absolute fan, ma'am,' he says to my companion. 'When is your next show? Does your Facebook page have a schedule?' My subject is certainly used to such adulation as she answers all his questions with her signature humility. 'That must give you a big high!' I say as the man walks away, admiration written all over his face. 'Huge. More than me, this gives a huge high to my parents, who now understand what it is that I do and why,' she says proudly.

What could be a better start to the meeting with Neeti Palta? She is that rare professional who gave up her corporate advertising job to first write for a children's TV show and then embarked on her chosen path: stand-up comedy.

Punctuated with acknowledgements from several people, our conversation soon seems more like a chat between friends than a first-time, formal interview.

I am curious to know what prompted her to choose such an unconventional career. 'As a child, what is your first memory of what you wanted to become?' I probe. Pat comes the reply, 'Vijay Jasoos. I am a huge Amitabh Bachchan fan. I walked around the house wearing a hat and shades, trying to solve non-existent mysteries.'

Brought up in an Army household, for Neeti, growing up meant going out for runs, taking in the aroma of a brand-new book as she sat down to read it, and spending time with her 'painful elder brother'.

She admits that her response to his bullying was to write 'nasty limericks' about him. She would recite them to him when he couldn't react, when he was in the washroom, for instance. This strategy no doubt honed her writing and running skills, for she went on to win several athletic championships, while writing , of course, became the mainstay of her career.

Her love for writing took her to a journalism school in Pune. Even before one traces her career journey, here is a personal tale that needs to be told in Neeti's characteristic humour. While in Delhi for a study tour, an uncle invited her for dinner. She recalls how the family fussed about her appearance, while she, 'too much of a tomboy', sat through it disinterestedly. Absolutely ignorant about the fact that a prospective suitor was around, she passed off the attention that a suited–booted gentleman gave her throughout the dinner as politeness. Until he asked her out for a walk. 'That is when the big realization dawned.' She chuckles. She also realized how one of his female relatives was trying to check her out as plausible daughter-in-law material and confesses that she was tempted to show her a missing tooth to indicate that she was a 'defective piece'. When she went back to Pune, she said no to the match, till her father took matters in his hands and convinced her to agree. Even then, what she remembers saying is, 'whatever', which was construed to be her consent.

The only way to go through the wedding, she says, 'was to pretend that it wasn't my wedding'. Apparently, even that pretence couldn't take her all the way, for the night before the wedding, bridal nerves were strong enough to force her to run away from home in her mehndi and chura. With the wedding rituals only hours away, 'panic' did not even begin to describe her mother's reaction. Her dad, however, knew that food was her solace in times of distress. Sure enough, they found her at KFC with a bucketful of chicken. If you think this is the end of the tale, no, not yet. On the day of the wedding, Neeti received a conventional gift with the most unconventional note—twenty-four red roses from her fiancé with a note that said, 'Please show up.' Show up she did and has been happily married, ever since.

Circling back to her career, the 'buzz' and vibrancy of the advertising world made her spend over a decade in the industry, rising through its ranks. With her designations came a lot of opportunities. As she succinctly puts it, 'When you hand out a business card that says Senior Creative Director, a lot of doors open up. Producers could be chasing, you could land up writing a film script and hobnobbing with film stars.' Not to mention the perks: a swanky office, flight mileage points—things that are all in a day's work for a jet-setting advertising executive.

Just when it was time to reap the benefits of having climbed up the corporate ladder, however, she decided to bid this life adieu. By her own admission, she could not 'continue to sell cola to the youth'. Probe her further and you realize there is a lot more behind this clever play of words. 'A doctor,' she elaborates, 'is left to make an intelligent diagnosis of the disease before he prescribes the medicines; but when you are a communication professional, it is the client who starts to tell you what you should do and how, because it is his money that is being spent.' 'If you are creative with "some level of self-respect", these things begin to get to you at some point,' she confesses.

The mad race for advertising awards cut no ice with her either. As the copywriter in her eloquently says, 'Being clever in my own space, not in real time, wasn't my yardstick of success. If with your campaign you upped on ground sales of the most shitty product, that is when you really deserve the award.' With that one sentence, she brings into sharp focus the whole debate of form versus function.

Neeti admits that it was a 'very big decision' to quit her job; explaining her decision to her parents, who had grown up with a world view that a good brand and stable income are the most important determinants of success, however, turned out to be a different ball game. They were absolutely against her decision; their initial advice was that if she wasn't finding the job challenging enough, she should just 'suck it up' and stay put. It was only when they saw her resolve that they relented. The one person who stood by her decision throughout was her husband, who, she tells me, has an indulgent smile on his face whenever she wants to try anything new. She quips how she often has to turn around and tell her husband *'ab main badi ho gayi hoon'* (I am a grown up now). Veiled behind this humour is the acknowledgement that he has been a 'pillar of patience' throughout her varied career choices.

Neeti had, at this point, attended a workshop held by Sesame Street, which was bringing a show called *Gali Gali Sim Sim* to India that promised to educate as well as entertain kids. Falling in love with the muppets at first sight, Neeti looked forward to playing a more meaningful career role: that of educating and entertaining the younger generation. For someone who had grown up with cartoons, and given her background in advertising, which had sensitized her to a lot of dos and don'ts, she sailed through the Sesame Street test.

The next three years were spent leading a team of writers at Sesame Street's small office—where six writers vied for one computer, a sharp contrast to her earlier job—and living her passion. It gave her a 'nice, fuzzy feeling' although she was working sixteen hours a day keeping the scripts flowing and the episode shoots underway. It was, as she says, 'exhausting yet exhilarating'.

It was around this time that the stand-up comedy circuit began to make its presence felt in India. The turning point came once again for Neeti when she attended a show of Colin Mochrie and Brad Sherwood of *Whose Line is it Anyway?* fame, when they toured India. When they needed a volunteer from the audience to make background sounds for a scene, Neeti was chosen. Soon, she was making such funny sounds that it had the audience in splits and the performers improvising scenes to match her sounds.

One week later, Neeti was at her first open-mike night, at an upscale restaurant in New Delhi; soon she grew to love these experiences so much that she was convinced to try another career switch. Only this time, it was harder to convince those around her. Her father was shocked—why a writer like Neeti would want to do this 'bhandpanti' was beyond him. Of course, today he is a changed man, and one of her biggest fans.

But before we reach this 'happily ever after' point, there's a lot of distance to be covered. This time, Neeti faced the fear of taking an untrodden path, of not having a stable pay, and in today's EMI economy, of not being able to pay EMIs! She recounts that around the same time, her husband, who had been with a large bank for over nineteen years, also quit his job to set up his own venture as a financial services distributor. They had just shifted into a new house and were paying two EMIs. But as she goes on to qualify, 'We both knew that with our reputations we could find a new job, but the idea was to do something that we enjoyed.' No one can put it better than her when she says, 'Beyond a point your "bullshit quotient" goes up and you need to find something that doesn't just give you money but also makes you happy.' You know you are not talking to someone who glorifies entrepreneurship for the sake of it when she tells you how, after her decision to turn full-time comedian, there was no work for months. While her husband's venture worked well, for a fiercely independent woman like Neeti, not earning herself came as a blow. For someone who was not used to looking at price tags, even paying Rs 200 at a coffee shop felt like a 'huge depletion' of her savings account. Besides, there were a whole lot of people who found her decision untenable in the first place and were waiting to be proven correct. She points out that there were times when she wondered if she had taken the leap in a fit of overconfidence. One is reminded of a line in Sheryl Sandberg's book *Lean In*: 'Despite being high achievers, even experts in their fields, women can't seem to shake the sense that it is only a matter of time until they are found out for who they really are—impostors with limited skills or abilities.'

With no success in her newly chosen field, Neeti felt just that: an imposter who had been found out!

Then came her first paid gig from a corporate through a friend, for a princely sum of Rs 5000. The butterflies in her stomach were suitably assuaged when, at the end of the fifteen-minute show, people told her that she had a flair for comedy and must pursue it. Today, Neeti has her hands full with corporate gigs, award shows and many other events. She recently performed at the Femina Women of Worth Awards 2015, a fitting platform for a woman like her. Admittedly, there are still people who don't understand the nature of stand-up comedy. But she is willing to let their comments go. She realizes how comedy has become synonymous with the new wave that has taken TV channels by storm. She is quick to remind you that while she isn't trashing that genre, that's definitely not what she does for a living.

Having come so far, she still had to show to her parents that what she did was something that they could be proud of. There came a golden opportunity when she was performing at the India Habitat Centre in New Delhi, a distinguished-enough setting to invite her parents over for a dekko. By this time she had gained enough experience to draw material from her own life and also to pick on her parents during the course of the show. Expectedly, the show was very well received. If she thought that the applause at the end of the show was fitting retribution, there was more to come. While she was waiting outside to head home, a family walked up to her to tell her how much they and especially their 'papaji' had enjoyed the show. 'Papaji turned out to be this 120-thousand-year-old gorgeous man who literally had roots growing under him,' Neeti says with a twinkle in her eyes. The high point came when papaji himself walked up to pat her and tell her how he will sleep *'ruj ke'* (contented) after having laughed so much. Neeti, whose parents were privy to the entire conversation, could see her dad's chest fill up with pride. That settled the matter.

The tone of light-hearted banter as we talk of her various stage shows and myriad experiences suddenly becomes a little solemn when she describes how comedy isn't all fun and games. The corporate assignments are sometimes 'soul-sucking' she says, as they insist on 'applying corporate principles to a comedian'. The briefs can be as stringent as 'Don't do anything controversial, don't do anything political, don't do anything religious', and as if for good measure, 'don't name anyone.' Her answer to them is matter-of-fact: 'Why don't you organize a *jagran* instead?' Comedy is meant to be 'irreverent', she says, and when this irreverence is stymied, the genre is being done a disservice. She is quick to qualify that there should be some corporate guidelines around the use of foul language, for example, but there cannot be a blanket ban on holding up a mirror to society.

Nothing matches the intensity of the discussion when it shifts to whether women comedians finally have a voice instead of pandering to the male world view. She admits to cracking jokes about herself, her childhood, and aspects that even she wasn't aware of till she got up on stage and spoke about them. That her life experiences provide grist for her mill can be seen in the jokes she makes around '*koi good news hai*' (any good news?), for example, and when she proclaims that the way to make babies is to keep two fruits on one's lap during a *jagrata*. This is something that she has obviously been subjected to many a time, especially after her decision to not have kids! Her craft, clearly, provides her with an opportunity for catharsis.

When asked whether choosing to do stand-up comedy was a covert revolt, against the fact that women are advised to be genteel and discouraged from taking up certain professions, she responds that she has always been too much of a tomboy to conform to stereotypes. However, she admits that when on stage, she finds herself cracking a lot of jokes about the stereotypes regarding women and is sometimes astounded and wonders where this angst comes from. One is reminded of Robin Williams when he said, 'For me, comedy starts as a spew, a kind of explosion, and then you sculpt it from there, if at all. It comes out of a deeper, darker side. Maybe it comes from anger, because I'm outraged by cruel absurdities, the hypocrisy that exists everywhere, even within yourself, where it's hardest to see.'

Broach the subject of discrimination in a profession that is predominantly male-dominated, and her voice jumps a notch.

'There are entrenched mindsets,' she says, confessing that her blood boils when people pander to stereotypes. She particularly recalls this all-girls' show *Women of Comedy* organized by *Hindustan Times* featuring performers such as Aditi Mittal, Mahabanoo Kotwal and herself. The previews on Twitter had slammed it with comments such as 'I don't want to go for chick comedy', a sexist nomenclature that she doesn't quite understand, especially since like any male comedian, women comedians too draw their material from all walks of life.

Just as one gets ready to slam societal stereotypes, she is quick to point out the flip side too. This time the reference is to a show by a male performer and a woman in the audience who, Neeti chuckles, 'defeats our purpose of fighting against female foeticide'. This lady sits with a checklist in her head deciding whether it is cool to laugh at a particular joke or to be offended at its sexist tone. Neeti rues that women are losing their sense of humour and becoming 'khaps of humour' instead. Her arsenal of jokes has quite a few quips on how feminism has become like jihad. Rest assured that while she says this, she has the innate capability of laughing at herself.

Picture this: Someone takes a dig at her that as she is a woman, she can take advantage of her gender. Pat comes her reply: 'Someone has to take advantage, it may as well be me.'

She explains how there are both pros and cons to being a female comedian. While she gets a lot of gigs because she is a woman, there are many shows that she point-blank refuses for this very reason; a dealer conference hosted in Bangkok, for example. She makes it clear that even if she is offered a handsome pay, she wouldn't take it because she isn't there to titillate. 'The Russian dancers will be a better bet,' she quips. As it is, she admits that being a woman comedian is enough for people to brand her as being 'easy'. With characteristic laughter, she tells me how with her short hair, she is often termed 'fast'. 'As if my short hair gives me some special aerodynamic quality.'

Her advice for wannabe female comedians is what comedian Tom Stade gave her when she started out. 'Neeti, no vagina,' he said, meaning that while on stage, she had to forget her gender and simply be a performer. This is one advice which has served her well, she admits.

Besides being a popular stand-up comedian, Neeti has also written the script for the Bollywood potboiler *O Teri*. She recalls how the story idea had come over a cup of coffee with a director friend. Soon they had developed it into a full-fledged script. When people told her that there were hundreds of scripts gathering dust on the tables of directors, she retaliated with, 'You cannot approach anything with that kind of mindset.' One thing led to another and the two found themselves in Mumbai narrating the script to Pulkit Samrat, who then wanted them to narrate it to none other than Salman Khan, his mentor. Salman Khan liked the script enough to ask his brother-in-law, Atul Agnihotri, to produce the film. *O Teri* didn't go on to become a super hit but surely Neeti has the ability to laugh that off too!

Her list of achievements is indeed impressive: She was voted Best Stand-up Comic at the Oz Fest; was India's first stand-up comedian to perform at Melbourne for the prestigious Melbourne Comedy Festival 2013; and was awarded the Devi Award instituted by the *New Indian Express*, in 2014.

It would be interesting to know, having come so far, what her thoughts are when she sees her contemporaries, who have stuck it out in the corporate rat race and have climbed several notches up the ladder. She admits to both a sense of nostalgia and redemption, with her characteristic honesty. 'Stand-up comedy,' she says, 'is a lonely business. You travel alone and perform among strangers.' She chuckles at how the childhood advice of not talking to strangers has now been turned on its head. 'Even though sometimes I miss the regular office buzz, on a Monday morning, when everyone else is facing the proverbial blues, I can choose to walk into a coffee shop and smell the coffee,' she reasons.

When asked what advice she would give to women sitting on the entrepreneurial fence, she first offers a word of caution. 'It is easy for me to sit on my high horse and say take the leap without knowing [anyone else's] ground realities.' But then, 'At some point of time, you owe yourself happiness and you will never know if it is possible till you try it,' she says. There is a sudden moment of truth, when she goes on to add that 'it is better to live with "oh shit" instead of "what if".' Now that is a line that sums up the voice of entrepreneurship and the voice of this book!

WORDS OF WISDOM

- 'At some point of time, you owe yourself happiness and you will never know it is possible till you try it.'
- 'You cannot approach anything with that kind of [negative] mindset.'
- 'Beyond a point your "bullshit quotient" goes up and you need to find something that not just gives you money but also makes you happy.'
- 'Stand-up comedy is a lonely business. You are travelling alone and performing among strangers.'
- 'Once I am up on stage, I am only a performer, not a man or woman.'
- 'It is better to live with "oh shit" instead of "what if"!'

Snapshot

Birth sign: Aquarius

Biggest role model: Kiran Bedi

Proudest moment: The look on my parents' face after seeing my stand-up show for the first time

Oft-repeated quote: 'Murphy is God, God is Murphy.'

Favourite downtime activity: Being a slave to my doggy

Most inspiring book/author: *Murphy's Law*

One big dream for tomorrow: World peace . . . If that takes time, then affordable plastic surgery.

Three must-haves for aspiring female entrepreneurs/creative professionals: A thick skin, sense of humour, sleeves that roll up easy

MALINI AGARWAL

aka MissMalini

Founder and blogger-in-chief, Missmalini.com

Founder:	MissMalini Publishing Pvt. Ltd
Past corporate avatar:	Worked as a Bollywood correspondent with BBC Asia; digital content head, Channel V; programming director and on-air presenter, Radio One; channel head, MTV Networks. Also writes a gossip column for *Mid-Day*.

Education:	Alumna of Delhi University
Just when you thought you had heard it all:	Started her career as a professional dancer

OPTIMIST PRIME

MissMalini is undoubtedly India's most famous blogger. If you are a Bollywood enthusiast, there is no way you could have missed her 'shiny, happy' take on movies, celebs, fashion, lifestyle and more. Riding the new wave of social media, she has interwoven her twin love for writing and Bollywood to create a powerful brand, Missmalini.com.

Few however know that her blog which has changed the world view of millennial Indians and captured their cool, multifaceted lifestyle, actually started out as a hobby. Sheer passion for her craft led her to quit her well-established career with some of the most prestigious media brands. Fittingly, she is today a media doyenne herself! From starting out on her living-room sofa doubling as her office to having four million unique monthly visitors, she has certainly taken her brand #tothemoon. This is her story.

'Ability has nothing to do with opportunity'—Napoleon Bonaparte, French military leader and emperor

A well-proclaimed social-media Jedi, there is hardly a step you can take in the digital world without bumping into MissMalini's ubiquitous presence. As I wait for our discussion to begin, I am curious to know how much of her online persona plays out in real life. A little into the conversation and it is amply clear that the brand MissMalini, an icon for today's youth, is very like her real-life counterpart—positive, sparkling, brimming with energy, and oozing charm and humour.

Courtesy her father's career as a diplomat in the Indian Foreign Service, Malini knew more about different cultures, fashion and lifestyle by the age of fifteen than most people do in a lifetime. Shifting home and hearth every three years meant growing up in countries as diverse as Somalia, Lebanon, Germany, Bulgaria, Greece and Ivory Coast before finally settling down in Delhi, India. 'That explains my funny accent,' she quips. As I ask her for her favourite stint, it is clear she can't bring herself to pick one. Nostalgia seeps through her voice as she describes the idyllic high school years spent at Ivory Coast, the old-world charm of Greece and the giant cherry tree in their backyard in Germany. There are some not-so-good memories as well, such as witnessing the horrific infighting in Lebanon from the window of her room and even innocently collecting bullet shells as a five-year-old.

As the youngest in the family (there is a gap of more than fourteen years between Malini and her eldest sibling), much of her childhood was spent hero-worshipping her elder brother and sister. They became her first role models and she remembers how for the longest time, she dreamt of fighting battles in courtrooms simply because her sister had taken up law as a profession.

An early interest in creative arts and languages led Malini to study English literature in college. She recalls how enrolling for an inter-college dance competition being choreographed by Ronica Jacob, a professional dancer, heralded the beginning of a career in dance. So impressed was Ronica by Malini's dancing skills that she made her an offer to join her dance troupe, Ronica Jacob and the Planets. Quick to take it up, Malini found herself thoroughly enjoying her job as a backup dancer for indie pop performers such as Sukhbir, Anamika and Shibani Kashyap. The highlight of her dancing career came when, in the year 2000, she had the opportunity to perform for the Channel V awards alongside music stars such as Peter Andre and Spice Girls who had flown down for the event

When quizzed on how her corporate career took off, she points out that while loving 'the physical energy of dancing', she found herself 'not so stimulated mentally'. The digital landscape had just started opening up and driven by her love for writing, she decided to pick up her first 'real job', as a content writer, at a newly launched portal covering Delhi city life. 'Writing has always been my hobby, right from an early age,' she says. 'I'll never forget the validation I felt when *Reader's Digest* published a poem I wrote when I was fifteen,' she adds. Nothing it seems is impossible in Malini's world, as she describes working as a copywriter during the day and doubling as a professional dancer in the evening for shows and events.

As I continue to trace her career journey, she tells me how the move from Delhi to Mumbai happened on a whim. Visiting a friend in Mumbai, she recalls how the city left her mesmerized. 'I found myself falling in love with its energy; I loved the neon lights and the fact that you could jump into a taxi (most probably with leopard-print upholstery!) at four in the morning feeling completely safe,' she says. The feeling of restlessness grew upon returning to Delhi and so Malini decided to herald the new millennium by moving to the city of her dreams. It is here that her career unfolded, much like a Bollywood film.

Starting off with a mere Rs 40,000 in her bank, she remembers sharing a room with 'six other girls and a pigeon' at a rent of Rs 625 a month. Her full-throated laugh fills the room as she says that the thought of the pigeon hitting the fan and covering her with blood provided enough motivation for her to chase her dreams with a vengeance, if only to be able to move out of that one-room set-up.

Her first job in Mumbai was with a tech start-up that built the Chalo Mumbai site for *Mid-Day*, which Malini later joined. She thereafter moved on to work at MTV India leading their web division as channel head for 'romance and sexuality'. There is a glint in her eye as she mentions how that nomenclature left many, including her mother, wondering what her daughter was up to in a new city. Wanting to give her creativity full reign, she also auditioned as an RJ at WIN 94.6 FM and came out a winner. 'Radio is the first love of my life. Radio made me realize for the first time how much I enjoyed being on air and interacting with people.' Malini enjoyed her radio stint so much that post WIN, she joined Go 92.5 FM where she continued as a radio jockey for eight years (and eventually turned programming director), hosting different shows like *Horn OK Please*, *225*, *Tiger Time with Malini*, *Overdrive* and *Malini till Midnight*. 'I particularly remember that on my show *Horn OK Please,* I would do a little dating game called Flirty @ 7.30 and set people up on-air; one couple actually ended up getting married as a result, imagine that!' she says animatedly. Alongside her radio gig came writing a gossip column called *Malini's Mumbai* in the popular tabloid *Mid-Day*. All of this while holding a day job!

As digital media continued to grow, so did her career, and she was soon working at Channel V as the head of digital content. Clearly hers was an enviable career path, one that she managed to carve by dint of her ability and passion for writing and interacting with people—talents that were waiting to duplicate themselves in another space, only that she didn't quite know it yet.

When asked how blogging happened to her, she replies with a disarming smile, 'My blog was an accident waiting to happen. It was while writing my gossip column that I discovered my love for Bollywood, fashion and lifestyle.' She remembers speaking to her friend Karan Wadehra about the limitations of writing a column: 'There is never enough space to write about everything I have seen or heard.' It was his casual suggestion to write a blog that went on to create virtual history. At a time when social media was just about making a beginning, her next question, 'But what is a blog?', opened the doors to a whole new parallel universe, one that she now rules with élan. She recalls how Karan showed her the hugely popular website perezhilton.com and she found herself completely hooked.

After seven years with millions of followers, her very first blog post still remains etched in her memory. She recalls a post about Rosa Catalano, Saif Ali Khan's ex-girlfriend, who was at a party where Malini also happened to be in attendance. Seeing her pose with olives and cheese set off a desire to pen down the 'cheesiness' of it on her blog. There's no mistaking the glint in her eye, as Malini describes the excitement of receiving those first few comments that brought home to her the power of the medium.

So how did she think of naming her blog MissMalini, which today of course is so well recognized? 'MissMalini comes from my name, and I added the "miss" to it, because one, it makes for a nice alliteration, and secondly, it symbolizes the young millennials around the world, as much as it stands for Indian youth kicking ass around the globe.' The blog continued to grow organically from there, as she offered readers her own unique take on Mumbai's party scene, movies and fashion.

Life took a different turn with the return of her then boyfriend and now husband, with a degree from Harvard Business School and a job in the financial services sector. Having seen the digital media explosion in the western world, he was quick to point out to her the possibilities of turning the blog into a profitable enterprise.

When asked how she finally made the mammoth decision of giving up a decade-old corporate career, which has a knack of becoming intrinsically entwined with one's identity, she keeps it very simple: 'I have always viewed myself as a creative professional and have never been hung up on [corporate] titles. In fact, throughout my corporate life, I have preferred being creative talent to management,' she says. As for managing household finances, the eternal issue that impacts many career crossover decisions, she recalls how she made good use of her ability to don multiple hats as she continued hosting events, radio shows and more to pay her bills, while working on her dream project. Married by now, she of course also had the support of her husband to take the leap towards entrepreneurship.

With a can-do spirit so characteristic of her, she details how, in 2011, for the first time in her adult life, she called it quits on her working life to focus exclusively on building a business model around her blog. That said, she admits that at the time of taking the leap she had decided that she would give her blog a shot 'for a year' to see how it shaped up. That year has turned into seven eventful years, with her blog growing from strength to strength.

When quizzed on the initial part of her journey, as she no longer had a fancy office to walk into every morning, she describes how 'my sofa became my writing seat' for over a year and the blog, 'a living, breathing extension of me, so if I didn't turn off, neither did the blog'. Looking back, she admits how it made perfect sense 'to distil all my industry experience and access in Indian entertainment and put it online'. Blogging became her way to share her experiences with a wider audience, and she did it with a charm and positivity that has made her a darling of her followers. As she honestly admits, 'I led two parallel lives, a virtual life and a real life, and I dedicated as much time and energy to my virtual life as I did to my real life.'

It was after a year of being curled up on the sofa of her living room, drawing up business plans with Mike Melli, a friend and business manager (who is now a driving force behind the business and the company's first and fiercely loyal employee), that she received her first round of funding. This in turn opened the doors even wider to a whole world of possibilities. When asked about the experience of being funded, she states, 'There were mixed feelings, joy at the fact that people had faith and were willing to put money in something that had been my baby from the very start. But there was also nervous excitement because I never thought of myself as a businesswoman and I wondered if that would take away from my creative time.'

Funding led to expansion and Malini moved from her couch to a proper office. Next came hiring a team of bloggers to launch a full-fledged website, a big step forward for an individual blog.

With a traffic of four million unique viewers and page views of over fifteen million a month, it's no secret that Miss Malini is today India's most influential blogger as she brings Bollywood titbits, behind-the-scene specials, the party circuit, fashion and lifestyle, all in Malini's signature 'happy, shiny' style. She's also a social media Jedi with 809K FB fans, 688K Twitter followers, and 139K Instagram followers (at the time of our interview and growing rapidly!) If you think Malini would now rest on her laurels, there is more.

'We realized we were creating content for different platforms, so why not for TV,' she says. A television show on TLC called *MissMalini's World* followed. Here too, she decided to go her own route rather than follow what has already been done to death. So instead of following the usual entertainment news show format where the host stands in front of the screen and talks about the latest gossip, Malini decided to adopt a more organic route. The show is literally an extension of MissMalini's World and aims to capture everything that goes on in Miss Malini's life. Cameras follow Malini wherever she goes, whether it is a fashion show or visit to a celebrity's house or even if she is travelling to Spain or New York for an event. The essence is to capture the sociocultural milieu surrounding the urban youth of India. As she says, 'Generally when people think of India, they think villages, they think *Slumdog Millionaire*. Nobody actually notices how much culture, enterprise, glamour and opulence there is. I want people to see what young millennial India is doing today! The millennial Indian will dance with reckless abandon at their best friend's wedding but at the same time loves global pop culture, technology, travel and social media as well!' The show has a huge fan base and will soon begin production on its third season.

The one thing, she admits, that has kept her going through her journey is the support that she has received from her husband and now business partner. They met during one of her Friday club meetings, a social group started by Malini during her early years in Mumbai as a means of getting like-minded people to share a drink and shake a leg together. She lays special emphasis on the fact that it was not meant to be a singles club or a dating club, although it has helped people including her find their life partners. It needs to be placed on record that as with everything else connected with her life, Malini had invited her online family to join in the wedding festivities with uploads of her wedding photos and blogs sharing details of the festivities.

Coming back to her work life, I am keen to know how working with her husband in the workspace has panned out and how she copes with differences of opinion at the workplace and their inevitable spillover into their personal lives. With a confidence that stems from understanding each other so well, she explains that it helps that he comes from a similar background and shares a world view that is compatible with hers. As a husband–wife duo, both work from a position of strength; while he oversees the commercial aspects, she handles the creative part of the business. It helps that their personalities are complementary, since 'you end up spending so much time together', she says. Besides she loves that he can make her 'split her side through the day' as she juggles her many roles. The latest addition to her repertoire is her role as an author. She is working on two books: the first, a sort of guide book for wannabe entrepreneurs on building a digital empire, a fitting book for someone who has had such a successful journey; the second, on a subject that she confesses she is obsessed with—'Love'. Her underlying big dream is to build a legacy brand that is able to make a name globally as a home-grown brand; one that endures well beyond her lifetime. Behind the hint of laughter is a whole lot of determination as she says that the cartoon MissMalini that she has created on her site, will 'age far better than I will'.

Amidst so much action, what does she do in her downtime, I ask. What I hear turns her into a poster girl for pursuing one's passion. 'The fact that I love what I do and do what I love makes downtime irrelevant,' she says. 'It is the perfect life for me. I love socializing, meeting people, travelling, which is what my job requires me to do as well; and so my job is not really like a job, it is a fantastic life.'

As I seek her advice for the new generation of bloggers, she says with her trademark candour, 'Find your passion, don't take to blogging for making money or to be famous, write or blog something that you love or you know. When you do that you will have no problem being successful.'

There is absolute conviction on her face as she asks wannabe entrepreneurs to 'Close your eyes and imagine what you would do for the rest of your life if no one paid you to do it. That's what your job should be and that will get you paid. We live in a generation where anything is possible, you can make anything your job as long as it is your dream and passion that is driving it.'

Malini is quick to cite her own example as proof that hard work and ambition can lead to success, effectively debunking in the process the popular cliché that you need a godfather to be able to succeed in a city like Mumbai. With only one friend in Mumbai and a mere Rs 40,000 in her pocket, it was her dreams and the willingness to give it her all that has led Malini to where she is today. That and her concept of 'entrepreneurial karma', which she explains has been one of her greatest learnings. 'People were always generous with me; they gave me a lot of love, advice and help as I began my journey. I try to do the same.' She is certain that 'If one helps people unabashedly, it will always come back.'

The slightly solemn tone that has set in is completely upturned as we suddenly start to chat about her favourite celebrity, among a host of them that she meets and covers every day. 'Oh I love them all,' she quips. 'I have been in love with Aamir Khan since I was nine years old. I told him that once and then realized that must have made him feel very old. I love these very talented and super self-made women as well, from Deepika Padukone to Priyanka Chopra.'

On this note as I bid this 'very talented and super self-made' person herself adieu, I cannot help but marvel at the incredible journey of a woman who started her career dancing in the shadows but is now occupying centre stage as her digital media footprints travel across the world. She may say that she has just 'been at the right place at the right time', but there is no denying the fact that she has given it her all to build a brand that is changing the paradigm for news and entertainment as we know it.

WORDS OF WISDOM

- 'Don't always look for something in return, help people unabashedly, give something of yourself and it will always come back.'
- 'Find your passion, don't take to blogging for making money or to be famous, write or blog something that you love or you know. When you do that you will have no problem becoming successful.'
- 'Close your eyes and imagine what you would do for the rest of your life if no one paid you to do it. That's what your job should be and that will get you paid.'
- 'We live in a generation where anything is possible, you can make anything happen, you can make your passion your job.'

Snapshot

Birth sign: Gemini

Role models: Adriana Huffington, Oprah Winfrey, Ryan Seacrest

Proudest moment: Being able to say that all the people who work for my company believe in the brand 'Miss Malini'

Oft-repeated quote: 'The greatest thing you will ever learn is just to love and to be loved in return'—Moulin Rouge

Favourite downtime activity: Checking my Instagram feed

One big dream for tomorrow: Leaving a legacy behind. One that people will look back and say that it accurately represents Millennial India. A home-grown brand to be proud of.

Three must-haves for aspiring female entrepreneurs: Confidence, energy, optimism

SONAM KALRA

Musician-singer, writer and composer

Founder:	Sonam Kalra & The Sufi Gospel Project
Past corporate avatar:	Art director/writer, Contract advertising, Trikaya Grey Voice-over artist (voice of Discovery Channel, IndiGo Airlines, and live voice host of the Commonwealth Games 2010) TV Anchor—BBC *Wheels*, BBC *The Real India Travel Show* and Star Plus *Musafir Hoon Yaaron*

Education:	Alumna of College of Art, New Delhi
Honours and awards:	L'Oreal Paris Femina Women of Worth Award 2015 for excellence in music and performing arts; Indian Express Devi Award 2014 for dynamism and innovation in music; Hailed as one of 'the 50 creative powerhouses' by *Mail Today* in 2013; Featured in the list of 'Transformers: Women Who Own the Future' by *Elle* magazine; Regular TEDx speaker
Just when you thought you had heard it all:	Won the META National Award for Best Actress for the play *Nati Binodini*

A SOULFUL RENDITION

It is not often that you come across someone who gives up a coveted job at a top advertising agency to pursue the love of her life—music. She then goes on to break new ground by creating a whole new genre of music through the Sufi Gospel Project to spread the message of oneness of all religions. In her own words, her music is 'living proof that many different Hallelujahs can exist in harmony'. That and much more is Sonam Kalra for you, a woman who lives by her philosophy of 'truth in the moment'.

Today her performances, where Amir Khusrau's words resound with 'Amazing Grace' and Kabir's dohas coexist with 'Abide with Me', dazzle audiences around the world. Her soulful journey began as she took a leap of faith with a three-month sabbatical from her job to pursue her love for music . . . never to look back.

'When I am silent, I fall into the place
where everything is Music'—Rumi, poet, scholar

The welcome, as I step into Sonam Kalra's home, is as warm as it can get. Rushing to me, love written all over, is her absolutely gorgeous canine, Gadbad! Not one to be satisfied with small measures of love, he jumps on to my lap while another lovely soul comes rushing up to me . . . and another . . . and another . . . and another. As I quickly find myself surrounded by five lovely dogs, the ongoing ruckus reminds me of a house filled with children. Their names are even more endearing—Gadbad, Chutney, Ladka, Ladki and Chhokra! This clearly is a dog lover's haven and an abode of unconditional love, five times over.

A few minutes into the discussion with Sonam and I start connecting with her sheer genuineness. She is a woman with the voice of a nightingale and the heart of a lion. How else would you describe someone with the rare capacity to turn life's challenges into soulful renditions? From the bloody carnage of the 1984 riots, her mother's relentless fight against and eventual surrender to cancer to the sudden death of her father and a dramatic career change—she has lived through it all, each experience reaffirming her belief in the essential goodness of humankind.

As she describes her childhood, I soon realize it couldn't have been any other way. With two incredible role models in her parents, there was a lot she picked up early. If from her mother's own passion for music and the arts flow Sonam's musical inclinations, to her father goes the credit for her never-say-die spirit. She still remembers a poster stating 'Don't Quit' that hung on her father's door, a testament to his unshakeable will to survive against all odds. Most importantly, from both her parents, she has learnt lessons about love, acceptance and equality, which are evident in the music she puts forth.

Growing up in a household where art and culture were greatly patronized, Sonam's early love affair with music was but natural. Her mother ran Shadaj, a music heritage society, and was largely responsible for fostering Sonam's love for music. Her eyes well up as she starts to recall the blissful childhood hours spent listening to Begum Akhtar's music, sitting on her mother's lap, on the very same chair that she occupies as I speak to her. Sonam's first music tutor was the younger of the famed Dagar brothers. His passing left a void too big to fill for an impressionable teenager and nearly severed her contact with music, at least for a while. Studies took centre stage thereafter, culminating finally in a degree in fine arts from the prestigious College of Art, New Delhi. This was followed by a stint in advertising where she lost no time in proving her mettle. Soon she was hankering for a bigger role in the creative process, not happy with the fact that she was being asked to art-direct ads that had already been conceptualized by the writer. Wanting to be at the genesis of the ideation process, she began writing her own ads, in addition to art-directing them. When it came to choosing between the lines written by her and the officially appointed writers, it was always her lines that made it to the final copy.

Agency protocol, however, demanded that she choose one of these two roles. 'People love to put you in boxes,' she tells me, and she hates it. In her scheme of things, if being labelled a writer meant she could be associated with the ad from the beginning of the ideation process, she did not mind exchanging the art director label that she had painstakingly acquired after four years of art school for that of a writer.

Her next assignment as a 'writer' was at yet another advertising biggie. Working with her usual dedication, she climbed the corporate ladder quickly, and awards and accolades for her work followed in rapid succession. It was also during this phase of corporate life that Sonam resumed her musical journey, this time training under legendary singer Shubha Mudgal. The long hours in advertising, however, did not leave her with much time to devote to music.

It was at the turn of the millennium, when everyone around her was making celebratory plans, that Sonam decided to give her life a fresh start. Encouraged by her husband and mother to study music, she requested her boss for a three-month sabbatical. She confesses how, at this stage, she didn't even know what she would do without a job, as until then all her waking hours had been devoted to her advertising career. Armed with her boss's assurance that she would remain on their rolls, to make it easy for her to come back should she wish to, Sonam proceeded on her sabbatical. Little did she know that she had taken her first, irreversible, step on her musical journey.

When quizzed on whether she had to battle the fear of giving up the familiar for the unknown, she says, 'I was quite clear about one thing, I have one life and I don't want to look back when I am seventy and say, I wish I had done that.' It is this ability to block out fear and find 'truth in the moment' that stood Sonam in good stead as she set out to explore newer horizons.

It did not, however, turn out to be a fairy-tale beginning to Sonam's musical career. What must be a singer's worst fear was realized when she lost her singing voice for almost a year to laryngitis and a series of throat infections, soon after quitting her job. Any other person might have been crushed by this impediment and chosen to return to their well-paying job, but Sonam is made of sterner stuff.

An opportunity to anchor *The Real India Travel Show* at BBC gave Sonam the break she was looking for and she took up the role with her usual panache. This was followed by other anchoring stints, including *Musafir Hoon Yaaron* on Star Plus. The fun part of her television career, though, came when as the host of the BBC show *Wheels*, she got the opportunity to test drive the swankiest of cars, effectively junking all stereotypes related to women and machines in the process. There is more than a hint of pride in her voice as she recounts an episode when she was pitted in a race against the famous rally driver Nikhil Taneja, who ended up complimenting her on her tremendous control and driving skills. With a mischievous smile, she goes on to mention how as a result of this show, no one dares say anything derogatory about women drivers in her presence!

Her voice fully recovered by now, Sonam once again devoted herself to music, travelling extensively for stage shows and concerts with her guru, Shubha Mudgal. The peaceful routine of her world, however, was shattered when her mother, whom she looked upon as her best friend, soulmate and anchor, was diagnosed with cancer.

The news that her mother was at stage four cancer, with four months to live, left Sonam and her family devastated, but determined to try everything to defeat the cancer. Referring to her mother as a 'Cancer Samurai', she tells me how it was her mother's positivity, strength, spirit and prayers that got the family through this difficult time. The pain of seeing her mother in and out of hospitals for chemotherapy, surgery and radiation left Sonam stressed and in need of an outlet. She recollects how, with a broken heart and her inability to sing, she decided to take up theatre to deal with the pain.

Perhaps even the gods were watching, for amazingly, within a week, she received a call to audition for the lead role in a play. Theatre welcomed Sonam, and not one to shy away from challenges, she went on to act in a number of productions, the most impactful and life changing being *Nati Binodini* by Amal Allana, one of her greatest teachers. 'Amal was an amazing director', she says, 'who taught us how to connect at the deepest level possible.' 'Above everything else, theatre helps you channel your emotions and makes you vulnerable yet stronger as you step out of your body and start connecting with the characters you play on stage,' she adds. She recalls a particularly poignant scene in *Nati Binodini*, where her character, a young girl, is being sacrificed to an older man in the ancient *bali* (sacrifice) tradition. Sonam felt so emotionally charged each time she was called on to act this particular scene that each performance was like her first, tears flowing at the plight of the young girl.

Even before I can ask her how she found such a strong connection to pain and the various other rasas, she tells me, 'There is no point in doing something, if you aren't feeling it from your core.' A philosophy that also explains why no matter what her career trajectory, she gave it her 100 per cent.

When quizzed about how she felt during this period when, despite her intervening successes, she hadn't fully achieved what she set out to after she left her corporate job, there is a world of wisdom in what she has to say: 'Nothing that I amassed in this period leading up to music was wasted. But for these experiences, I wouldn't be what I am.' There are no regrets about the time it has taken her to reach her destination, for she has learnt something precious from each and every experience. 'The ride,' she says, 'has been well worth it.'

Her voice fills with respect as she talks about Amal, who taught her an invaluable life lesson that she reminds herself about every now and then: 'As long as there is truth in your performance, even when there is imperfection, there will always be beauty.' You can hear the same philosophy echoing in her music, which is perhaps why her audience feels such a deep emotional connection with Sonam every time she sings.

Sonam clearly has considered a number of roles before coming 'home' to music. 'My mother is the reason I sing,' she says, looking heavenwards. Although she bid adieu to advertising in 2000, it was not until 2006 that her first musical performance, a veritable mix of jazz, Broadway and gospel music, took place at the prestigious India Habitat Centre in New Delhi, with her mother seated proudly in the front row of the audience. With an auditorium packed to capacity and an appreciative audience enjoying every moment of the concert, Sonam could not have asked for a better beginning to her musical career. A roaring ovation at the end, coupled with the look of contentment and unbridled joy on her mother's face even though she was battling cancer, put Sonam firmly on the path to her destiny. This show remains a proud moment for her.

Invitations to sing at musical events and festivals soon followed. The fact that a Sikh girl could sing gospel (read, Christian hymns) so beautifully intrigued people. When asked how she did it, Sonam's answer remained the same: 'God has no religion and religion isn't God, and I should be allowed to call out to Him in whichever way it feels true to me.'

An invitation to sing gospel music at the Urz (birth celebration) of the Sufi saint Inayat Khan turned out to be a defining moment in her life, laying the foundation for the Sufi Gospel Project. It was an honour beyond belief for Sonam, and she decided to use the opportunity to blend Sufi and gospel music to convey the message of oneness and secularism. Her soulful renditions created a magical evening, doing justice to the momentousness of the occasion.

When asked about the first show of the Sufi Gospel Project, she admits that there were doubts in her mind, especially as she was attempting to redefine Sufism in some ways, making a unique, contemporary, all-inclusive definition and breaking traditional boundaries with her new style and ideology. In her own words, 'The Sufi Gospel Project is an effort to blend all the voices of faith, through the use of song, music and the spoken word.'

The first Sufi Gospel project show surpassed even her wildest expectations. She recalls a moment of pin-drop silence in the audience after everyone had stopped clapping, when a graceful lady walked up to her and said in a voice loud enough for everyone to hear, 'My dear, straight from your lips to God's heart.' Those words are etched forever in Sonam's mind; it was as if her mother, who had passed away by then, had come down to bless her concert. From then on, she considers every performance a prayer, bringing her closer to God and her parents.

There have been many such experiences since, with people walking up to her with tears in their eyes, baring their souls after listening to her music. A Christian keyboard player, Muslim sarangi and tabla players, a Hindu flautist and herself, a Sikh, Sonam believes this ensemble is further testament to the message she is trying to convey through her music.

While hers seems like an extraordinary journey for someone who started out with a traditional corporate career, it is indeed her intrinsic ability to be true to herself and her calling that led her so firmly on to the path of her destiny. Shubha Mudgal had once told her that 'to sing you have to have lived'. And lived Sonam has, in full measure. Her music is alive with experiences drawn from her life; as the youngest in the house, Sonam spent many a night during the 1984 riots holding on to her mother, the fear of the unknown weighing down upon her. But even then her parents didn't let those feelings of fear cloud her understanding of equality and acceptance of all people and faiths.

Today, it is with this belief in the essential goodness of people and her deep faith in humanity that she uses her soulful voice to espouse the causes she strongly believes in. She has lent her voice to many fundraising concerts for diseases such as cancer, multiple sclerosis and thalassaemia as well as for issues such as education for the underprivileged and for women's rights, a cause very close to her heart. After all, this is the woman who grew up hearing from her father that 'women are not equal to men, they are better'. She speaks passionately of how women have an 'intrinsic wisdom' and all they need to do is to reach into their core to find so many answers.

As for herself, she has truly found her own answers in music. Music has bestowed on her both national and international fame and recognition, and has taken her to venues such as the Pyramids in Egypt, the Nehru Centre in London, the Chicago Temple Building in the USA and Amber Fort in Jaipur, to name a few.

Success rests easy on her shoulders; life for her stays very much within the simple boundaries defined by her connection to music and her rock-solid relationship with her husband of eighteen years, Aditya. When asked what she admires the most in him pat comes the response, 'His integrity and honesty.' She admits that she is lucky to have found him. 'They don't make men like him anymore.'

As someone who has repeatedly broken new ground, her advice to women who are sitting on the entrepreneurial fence is that when it comes to taking that leap, worrying about whether you will sink or swim is what holds us back; the reference to the seismic change she was able to bring to her own career by not falling prey to fear is, unmistakable.

'Stop worrying and just do it. It is intrinsic to our nature to survive. You will swim,' she says, determination writ large on her face. Drawing from her own early experiences, she adds, 'You may feel like you have jumped into an abyss at first, but before you know it you will end up carving your own path and learning so much more about your own self. All you need to do is open yourself up to experiences.' 'But do whatever you must for the right reasons,' she cautions. She herself sings with passion and is clear that the day she starts to sing for commercial success alone, 'It won't work in my own head and won't make a connection with the audiences.'

As I get ready to bid her adieu, I realize it is not often that one sees true passion that has remained unaffected by success; but therein is the true essence of being Sonam—a 'Soul Sensation'. For her, however, she is 'just Sonam trying to be the best that she can be'.

WORDS OF WISDOM

- 'Where there is truth, there will always be beauty, even when there is imperfection.'
- 'To be able to sing, you have to have lived.'
- 'Don't look back when you are seventy years old and say I wish I had done that, do it now!'
- 'Women are not equal to men, they are better.'
- 'If you do not feel pain, you will never know joy.'
- 'All you ever need to be is yourself.'
- 'Strive to be the best version of yourself that you can be, don't imitate.'
- 'Stay humble. Humility is one of the greatest virtues you can have.'

Snapshot

Birth sign: Aquarius

Role models: My parents; they are and will always be my strength and greatest sources of inspiration.

Proudest moment: When I shared the stage twice with the legendary Abida Parveen at Jahan-e-Khusrau. And when I won two awards for excellence in music and performing arts.

Oft-repeated quote: 'I want to sing like the birds sing, not worrying about who hears or what they think'—Rumi

Favourite downtime activity: Playing with my five amazing dogs and spending time with my husband

Most inspiring book/author: Rumi, Kabir and Bulleh Shah

One big dream for tomorrow: To sing at the Fez Festival in Morocco, perform at WOMAD, and one day at the Royal Albert Hall. To continue doing music for the rest of my life as prayer, worship, and ibadat, with honesty, truth and integrity.

Three must-haves for aspiring female entrepreneurs/creative professionals: There are four—confidence, faith, optimism and the will to work hard.

SAIREE CHAHAL

Social entrepreneur

Mentor and founder, Sheroes.in

Founder:	www.sheroes.in
Past corporate avatar:	CII, A and M Magazine, Heidrick and Struggles
Education:	Alumna of Jawaharlal Nehru University, New Delhi
Honours and awards:	Cartier Women's Initiative Asia-Pacific Finalist 2012; Sunday Standard Devi Award 2014;

	Featured as one of the most powerful women in India Business Today 2012; Femina Powerlist North Awardee, 2015; TEDx speaker
Just when you thought you had heard it all:	Author publisher—*Small Town, Big Dreams*

SHERO OF SHEROES

When you aim as high as Sairee Chahal, breaking new ground comes naturally! She was the first woman in her extended family who stepped out of her small-town home to pursue a corporate career. To the dismay of naysayers who construed her self-assuredness as overconfidence, she then went a step further and took on the role of an entrepreneur.

Driven by the passion and belief that women have an equal right to financial independence, she launched the hugely successful Sheroes.in (started as Fleximoms). Today she has turned into a role model for thousands of women who are seeking to re-enter the workforce, as she offers access to a number of flexible employment models. Her next goal is to touch the lives of 1 million women over a period of three years. To read Sairee's story is akin to gulping down inspiration in large doses.

'Life does not give us purpose; we give purpose to life'—Bartholomew Allen, Fictional Superhero

'A big canvas to paint on' is what she yearned for, growing up in small-town Muzaffarnagar. With thousands of women finding their calling and re-entering the workforce through her labour of love, Sheroes.in, today the canvas is not just big, it is indeed colossal.

When I meet Sairee at the India Habitat Centre, the first thing that strikes me about this petite, self-assured woman is her incredible drive. Slender, not a hair out of place, there's single-minded focus oozing out of her very persona. Sitting to speak with her, I find myself instinctively charmed by her soft-spoken personality. Only, beneath the charming personality lies an iron resolve. There is no mistaking the determination in her eyes when she talks about the topic closest to her heart—reconnecting more and more women with their careers!

The elder of two sisters, her fondest childhood memories are of spending long leisurely hours reading, lying on the grass or under the shade of a tree. Books opened the eyes of young Sairee to the world outside and gave wings to her dreams for the future. What books also brought home was a rather painful realization at the time—the fact that she was wired differently from the rest of her extended family. 'The wavelengths never matched,' she confesses. The favourite topic of discussion among the female members of her clan revolved around discussing their shopping escapades, and young Sairee found herself totally uninterested in discussing what she terms the 'superfluities of life'. Enamoured by the unlimited opportunities the world had to offer, she began a journal to note down all that she wanted to accomplish as a grown-up, her very first 'bucket list', so to say. 'Being an entrepreneur topped the list even back then,' she says (journalism and sociology are some of the others that made it to her list!). 'The problem with me is that I wanted to do too many things and all at the same time,' she quips. What is remarkable and truly inspiring about Sairee is the fact that she has managed to tick off most items on that bucket list, a feat very few of us can boast of.

Growing up at a time when career was equated with being a doctor or an engineer, Sairee's school, like many others, offered students only the option to study science after class ten. Quite a trailblazer even at the time, she remembers walking up to the principal to request him for a commerce and humanities stream as well. While humanities got an outright rejection, the principal agreed to introduce the commerce stream, thereby allowing Sairee to opt for electives of economics and commerce.

Feeling suffocated in the small-town environment (whose aspirations she terms as 'different') led her to explore schools outside her home town right after class ten. This led to some heated discussions with her father, who was not willing to let his daughter venture out alone into the world, at least not yet. 'The vision of running away very quickly to a world of possibilities was very strong,' she says with her trademark focus. Though he managed to hold his daughter back then, he was forced to give way to her insistence when she got admission to the prestigious Jawaharlal Nehru University (JNU), New Delhi, to study international languages; there has been no looking back since then.

Self-assured even back then, she does not remember ever doubting her ability to survive in a big city like New Delhi. While many dubbed her 'overconfident', in reality, her confidence stemmed from a firm hold of her priorities. In fact, she credits much of her success to her ability to block out all unwanted distractions, to leave time only for the essentials. It has served her well right from her early college days when she would leave her hostel in the morning to attend her classes, driving straight to work from there, her old Fiat for company. Even today her calendar is consciously split between work time and downtime and has her husband quipping that he sees her either 'working away furiously on the laptop or practising yoga'. A rather 'horse-headed' view of life as she herself says, but then that is what it takes to be Sairee Chahal.

The urge to earn her way through college took her barging into the office of the editor of an advertising magazine to 'demand a part-time job'. Her logic, impeccable—that her college was right across the road! 'Bending rules has always been in my DNA, it didn't even strike me at that time that this is not the norm and these people are big shots,' she says with her characteristic confidence. One can only imagine what the editor's thoughts must have been, agree as he did to appoint her, impressed by her self-assurance.

From writing for a magazine to working for the CII and even working with a blue-chip consulting firm, Sairee has never been one to stick to the conventional path to success. She recounts how at the young age of twenty-three, a casual meeting with Deepak Kamran, an ex-mariner, gave her what she calls her 'first taste of blood as an entrepreneur'. With first-hand experience of how desperately mariners longed to receive news from back home, Deepak was keen to launch a news magazine for mariners at sea. By the end of the discussion, he not only ended up inviting her to launch a newspaper, but also handed over the keys to his empty apartment to set up as an office. Convinced of Sairee's ability to deliver, Deepak even agreed to bankroll the entire operation till it could fund itself. Both touched and excited by his faith she took on the challenge with panache.

The next day saw Sairee at the apartment, geared to set up what would turn out to be the highly successful *Newslink Services*. With over twenty-five issues in three years, *Newslink Services* managed to capture two-thirds of the market globally—a success from the word go. By the end of three years, what began as a small operation evolved into a robust team comprising more than sixty editors and translators. That was Sairee's first tryst in the start-up space, one that was waiting to be duplicated in another time and genre.

As I continue to trace her career history, I am taken in by the imagery of this young girl with no role models up close to guide her. In fact, as a first-generation professional-turned-entrepreneur she recalls how she could never have a conversation back home about her work life, as everyone had very different aspirations. 'How long can one talk about kitty parties?' she asks; only it is a rhetorical question for a woman with such single-minded focus. 'When it came to discussing work it was,' she says, a 'blank wall'; a wall that she chiselled to perfection, so much so that now she is happy to play role model to not just her cousin's children but also a whole generation of other women. 'Had I chosen to stay back', she says, 'it would have been a very different life.' She remembers a recent visit to meet her parents, where her father in a light-hearted vein, tried to picture her life had she not broken out of the family mould. His image of Sairee married to a bureaucrat and serving chai to guests, stands in sharp contrast to the substance and direction she has managed to give her life.

It was during her stint at a blue-chip consulting company that Sairee for the first time experienced the cons of working within a formal organizational structure with defined processes and systems. Feeling stifled, the longing to be her own boss grew into an irresistible calling. When asked if she experienced fear in giving up the stability of a corporate job, she says, 'I always knew that I would not last in a corporate job for a long time, even when I was twenty. Only the specifics of it were not clear to me at the time. I knew that I wanted a larger canvas. When I set up my own consulting company, it was homecoming of sorts.'

She admits that as always there were people who were quick to dismiss her plunge into entrepreneurship as a mistake born out of 'overconfidence'. Regardless, she went ahead based on a gut feeling which was 'like a radar guiding you even though you might not fully understand it then'.

It was with the launch of SAITA Consulting in 2006, that Sairee took to the quintessential larger canvas. Named after the founders, Sairee and Anita, SAITA did well operating as a general management consulting firm focused on small and medium businesses (SMBs). As a flexible employer, SAITA received many applications on a daily basis from women desperately looking for opportunities to re-enter the workforce, this despite the fact that SAITA operated with a small twenty-member team and was not actively hiring. The huge influx of résumés set Sairee thinking. Giving birth to her own daughter around the same time made her realize how childbirth can cause many women to put their career on the back burner. 'Why go too far,' she quips, 'at my own high school reunion, out of a class of sixty with thirty-five girls, only five were working. And nobody found that odd!'

She was clearly intrigued by the employment dichotomy that needed bridging; on the one hand organizations were struggling with shortage of skilled manpower, while on the other hand thousands of skilled experienced women were seeking work opportunities that allowed them to balance family life with work. With the firm belief that equality in a relationship is possible only if both partners possess equal financial power, she decided to take up the issues of women and their careers, especially their second chance at working life.

When asked what her initial journey was like, she recalls that as a very nascent concept back then, flexible working did not enjoy credibility among business leaders. Corporate folklore has always been rich with tales of interview questions for women revolving around their plans of starting a family, as that is considered the end of the road as far as their careers are concerned.

Having launched and managed a successful start-up, Sairee knew from experience that both businesses and women jobseekers could benefit from alternative work models. The expanding universe of the Internet was at the time transforming the business landscape, making global virtual teams and remote working practical workplace realities. Not one to let a golden opportunity pass by, she took it upon herself to find a workable means of making job opportunities accessible to thousands, indeed lakhs of women wanting to restart their careers without sacrificing family life. A stickler for perfection, she started a pilot run with some of her consulting clients. To her credit, she managed to get past the apparent scepticism to convince at least some businesses to give flexible working a trial. The rest, as they say, is history. 'All I did was provide a platform for women returning to work to explore opportunities that fitted in well with their family life,' she says humbly.

When quizzed on her own journey as a woman entrepreneur, she admits, 'In the start-up space you are expected to be young, male and an engineer and since I didn't fall into any of these categories I wasn't so easily accepted.' She recalls how often she found herself the only woman in all-male gatherings. Not one to cower down when it comes to asserting herself in a male-dominated set-up, she remembers attending a conference where someone brought up the question of what her husband thought of her entrepreneurial venture. Her instantaneous reply was 'When was the last time you asked a man what his wife thought of his career choices?' much to the shock of the audience.

Speaking of her husband, I am keen to know how they came together. She explains that they met during her advertising stint. He was the blue-eyed boy of the company known for his impressive bylines and a penchant for winning awards. 'Most importantly he wasn't an MCP,' she quips, turning the scales pretty much in his favour. Apparently food proved to be a great leveller. 'As he was staying out of home and I was a hosteller, our common aim in life was to find good food,' she jokes. The good-hearted laugh that follows suddenly gives way to a strong admission that she is happy to have found two 'fiercely independent' women in the form of her mother- and sister-in-law.

Sairee is definitely not your stereotypical woman—serial entrepreneur, mentor, flexiwork evangelist and mother. When asked which of her multifarious roles that she plays defines her best, the fact that she chooses to be defined as an entrepreneur over everything else gives you a hint of the passion that keeps her charged. With humility, she describes the recognition and her various awards as 'an affirmation of the change you have sought to bring about in society towards encouraging women at work.' With Sheroes.in having closed a round of angel funding lately, Sairee is all geared up to leave no stone unturned in further perpetrating this change.

While mentoring female professionals is all in a day's work for her, what would she specifically want to tell women who are sitting on the entrepreneurial fence being nudged by myriad fears, I want to know. 'Be kind to yourself and follow your inner voice. It is almost never wrong though it can throw you out of your comfort zone. We are so defined by other people's idea of success that our inner voice gets drowned,' she says.

Coming from someone who has always followed her instincts, her advice is apt, 'There is no perfect formula for success. Stay grounded to who you are and build your own road map.' Not many work with this self-assured view of life—but then not many can turn their life around as she has, or that of so many other women.

WORDS OF WISDOM

- 'Build your own life, map your road, and go by gut feeling; it is like a radar guiding you even though you might not fully understand it then.'
- 'Be kind to yourself and follow your inner voice. It is almost never wrong though it can throw you out of your comfort zone.'
- 'We are so defined by other people's idea of success that our inner voice gets drowned.'
- 'Stay within the Simple Zone.'
- 'Say no, when it does not work for you.'
- 'There is no formula for success; you need to build your own roadmap for success.'
- 'Sign of a good social impact is that when you are no longer required and you can move on to solve a different problem.'

Snapshot

Birth sign: Leo

Biggest role model: Anu Aga, Anita Roddick, Dr V. Kurien, Elon Musk

Proudest moment: Serving the first million career requests at Sheroes.in

Oft-repeated quote: 'The most common form of despair is not being who you are'—Søren Kierkegaard

Favourite downtime activity: Yoga and spending time with family

Most inspiring book/author: *Little Prince*

One big dream for tomorrow: 100 million women as part of GDP creation process

Three must-haves for aspiring female entrepreneurs: Consistency, learning and 'Can do, Will do' attitude

MONICA BHIDE

Food and fiction writer

Published works:	*Modern Spice, The Everything Indian cookbook, The Spice is Right, The Devil in Us, A Life of Spice*
Past corporate avatar:	Worked in corporate America for thirteen years including stints with Ernst & Young and Hewitt Associates
Education:	Alumna of George Washington University

Honours and awards:	Published in top-tier publications including *Food and Wine*, the *Washington Post* and the *New York Times;* Named by the *Chicago Tribune* as one of the seven food writers to watch out for in 2012; Mashable.com picked her as one of the top ten food writers on Twitter, in the same year
Just when you thought you had heard it all:	Speaker and teacher, the Smithsonian Museum

A LIFE OF SPICE

When you have a degree in engineering from Bangalore University followed by two Master's degrees from top-notch US universities leading to a corporate job with a six-figure salary, you have all that it takes to be termed 'successful'. But not when you are Monica Bhide.

Shaken by the experience of losing her best friend, she sat down to write her own obituary and realized that more than anything else, she wanted to be known as a 'writer who told stories of hope and inspiration'. This realization led her to throw in the towel on her decade-long career in corporate America and become a writer. Sure enough, there were a host of naysayers to whom her only response was, 'It isn't a choice, but a calling.' Today her body of highly acclaimed work has silenced her critics. This is her story of belief and passion.

'Art is eternal, but life is short'—Evelyn de Morgan, English painter

Picture a fifth-grader being asked to write an essay about a spring morning. The last thing you would expect is a write-up about a war-torn country with a mother crying over her dead son on the street. The teacher didn't expect it too and true to the belief that a spring morning is supposed to be happy, gave a zero for the essay. The child walked up to the vice principal, who marked the essay an A+, but not before reminding the child that she had a powerful voice that must be used to voice diverse opinions.

That is Monica Bhide for you. The fifth-grader who has grown up since, but the one thing that has remained unchanged is her powerful voice. One would think, for someone with such a vivid imagination and exceptional writing skills, her career as a writer would be cut out early. Not quite. 'It's been a hard road to get here,' she says.

Having left India when she was just six, she grew up in the Middle East. As a child of immigrant Indian parents, attending school regularly and getting good grades was a given. But so was her love for food and stories, a concoction that she used to her advantage in later life. Her father used to travel a lot and his return was always an occasion for celebration, with stories about the food that he would bring back from different countries.

When she graduated from high school, she wanted to study journalism and even received a full scholarship to a university in California. But her father, with a mindset that is common to most migrants, felt that a technical degree would offer his daughter greater financial security and persuaded her likewise. Monica ended up studying engineering in Bangalore and followed it up with two master's degrees from the United States, one in information systems technology and the other in industrial systems management, culminating in a thriving corporate career.

Her job with a consulting company, teaching project management and leadership skills, by her own admission 'paid good money and got me to see the world'. She recalls how much pride her parents took in her career progression and how many Indian parents would reach out to her in the United States, seeking career advice for their daughters as they wanted them to 'become like her'. While she dished out helpful career tips, she secretly hoped that these girls would go on to follow their own calling instead of emulating her.

Clearly, from any outside perspective she had a lot going for her—a thriving career and a great marriage. Speaking of marriage, here is one endearing tale of the universe conspiring to get two people together. She tells me how as a young student all of twenty-one, she had just about arrived in the United States for her master's degree, when the Gulf War broke out. Homesickness, magnified with worry for her family in the Middle East, didn't make for a pretty tale. One day, her anxious state further heightened by the sound of gunshots in her neighbourhood, she set out to make kheer—comfort food in more ways than one, as it reminded her of her mom and the warmth of home.

A young Indian student, Sameer Bhide, whom Monica had only briefly met in college before, happened to be passing by and stopped to console her. Having assured her that the sound of gunshots was only from a bunch of kids playing with toy guns, he stayed back to dig in to the delicious kheer! Twenty-two years on, he continues to dig in to the kheer she makes with the same fervour and she doesn't hesitate in admitting that as with everything else in her life, food has had an important role in their union.

While totally fulfilled on the personal front, she felt herself getting into a rut when it came to her professional life. After having spent nearly thirteen years in the corporate world, Monica had this nagging feeling that she wasn't doing the kind of work that would 'leave behind a legacy'. In fact, at times she even remembered feeling that her job had become some kind of a 'golden handcuff' that gave her a lot and yet took away a lot more.

It is at this time that her existence was shaken by the news of the death of her German friend Beth Lipka. Her animated voice tells you how Mike and Beth Lipka were the first couple Sameer and she had become close to post marriage. Beth was an incredibly talented lawyer and despite the fact that Beth and she were very different people—Beth had no taste for Indian spices, and she for German beer—they grew to love each other dearly. After the birth of her baby, Beth quit her high-paying job to make time for the baby as well as to pursue her dream of working with a non-profit organization to give back to society in a meaningful way. There's palpable nostalgia in Monica's voice as she remembers her last conversation with Beth on the subject of quitting her job only to be told unequivocally, 'You get only one chance to do what you love.' Soon after, Monica and her family moved to Washington DC and life continued in much the same way till they got a heart-wrenching call from Mike one morning. Apparently, Beth was on her driveway, rollerblading with her young son when she fell and hit her head on the sidewalk. She remained on life support for a very short time before passing away.

The suddenness of her departure left Monica shell-shocked, to say the least. Beth was all of thirty-five and her life had been abruptly cut short without notice, with as little as an innocuous fall.

The last conversation with Beth kept playing over and over in Monica's head. It was almost as if Beth had had a premonition of things to come. The episode shook Monica so much that she remembers sitting down to write her own obituary to probe into what she would like to be remembered for. While she came up with the obvious list first—being a good mother and wife, further probing brought out her desire to leave the world a better place. A cause that wasn't being furthered by her professional choices, she felt. Deep down, Monica knew that her heart lay in telling stories that made a difference, however small. She wanted to speak of life as a parent, use food as a lens to examine life, share her experiences as a wife, explore mythology and so much more. And yet, the sceptic in her cautioned her against being whimsical. 'Did art really matter?' the voice asked. The answer that she got from herself was a resounding 'YES'. That, for her, made the decision.

Armed with this new-found perspective, she mustered the strength to submit her resignation at her coveted job. She recalls telling her husband that evening that she had 'cut the family income by half'. When asked if she had feared giving up the identity she had carved for herself, she says, 'Fear came later, when I realized what I had done. At the time that I resigned, I felt calm and happy as if a burden was being lifted. It was not really a choice. It was a calling.'

She agrees, though, that the aftermath of quitting was immense. While she herself was reeling under the fear of how she would pay her monthly bills, there was the added pressure of a lot of people close to her who felt that her decision was untenable. In fact, she recalls several interactions with Asian friends who felt that she had been extremely fickle in giving up a decade-old career. It was hard for her to explain that in choosing to write, she was not just choosing a new career, she was in fact giving voice to her identity.

Of all the people affected by her decision, her mother took it the hardest. 'To watch her highly qualified daughter with multiple educational degrees and a thriving career give it all up, that too to cook chicken curry or write about it', Monica says with a chuckle, 'wasn't easy.' Besides, her mother was the one left facing an army of friends and relatives with the inevitable question, 'Your daughter did WHAT?'—the idea that anyone can be naïve enough to quit a well-paying job 'just like that' was alien to them. Except that Monica's decision to quit was not made 'just like that'. The 'risk', she admits, was huge but, in the same breath, she says that there was this feeling that if it was right for her, a 'safety net would appear on its own'. The two people who offered unstinting support at this time were her husband and her father. Her father had turned sixty that year and Monica remembers writing to him, telling him of her decision. His prompt response assured her that if this indeed made her happy, she had his blessings.

While still in her job, Monica had indulged her love for cooking and writing by contributing articles to eGullet, a forum dedicated to the advancement of culinary art. Food writing had not emerged as a genre of its own back then, and writing about food did not generate the kind of celebrity status it does today. Yet, there were a number of food enthusiasts including the likes of Chef Bourdain, who went on to acquire his celebrity status much later, who shared their food-related thoughts on the site. Monica's articles centring on life, with food as a lens, got a lot of traction in terms of followers. But that was then.

Just now, having bid adieu to her corporate life, she decided to take a short vacation to India. On this holiday, she remembers praying a lot for a sign from God that would point her in the direction of her new vocation. Sure enough, she found her answer when she got back to the United States. A well-meaning friend had entered a few of her food essays from eGullet for a competition and she had been adjudged the Voice of The Year in food writing. If this wasn't a sign, what was?

Amidst all this talk about food, I ask her what it is about food that drives her to write so articulately about it. Promptly comes her good-humoured reply, 'I am a Punjabi. It runs in my blood.' She admits though that the switchover to full-fledged writing had its own hiccups. She remembers attending a conference focusing on the craft of writing and being absolutely mortified with the technicalities being discussed. Being an engineer by education, she had just no idea about the jargon being thrown thick and fast at her—query letters, masthead, lead and more. Such was her overwhelmed state that a fellow attendee, whom Monica describes as a 'beautiful American with a short blunt pixie haircut', turned towards her to ask her why she looked so upset. A dazed Monica told her how she had quit her job to write and now how ill-equipped she seemed for the task, given the intricacies being discussed. She sparked enough interest in the lady for her to ask Monica what is it that she wanted to write about. What she got in return was an impassioned monologue on how she wanted to cover an Indian wedding from the food perspective. 'Why don't you write for us,' said the American lady. 'And you are . . . ?' asked a slightly embarrassed Monica. The lady turned out to be the food section editor with the *Washington Post*. This was the proverbial deus ex machina in operation or in true blooded Bollywood style '*agar kisi cheez ko dil se chaho toh puri kayanat use tumse milane ki koshish mein lag jati hai*'. And to write is something that Monica wanted to do more than anything else.

Today Monica's writings have appeared in top-tier media, including *Food and Wine, Bon Appétit,* the *Washington Post,* the *New York Times, Ladies Home Journal* and many others. Her articles are as much about food as a slice of life! Sample this: 'My father would teach me to roast spices and learn that coriander whimpers, cumin smoulders, mustard sizzles and cinnamon roars. I learned to cook by sight as the colours of the spices turned and then by smell—sweet, earthy, heady, sharp if they are roasting correctly, or the unforgiving acrid smells if they burn. My mother taught me to make curries by hearing how onions sing in oil, from a slight sizzle to a glorious harmony as they get perfectly caramelized. I learned to watch the tomatoes marry the onions. The sign the union was complete and ready for spices to be added was when the oil separated from the mixture.'

With her compelling stories about the relationship between food, family and culture, it is little surprise that she was named as one of the seven food writers to watch out for by the *Chicago Tribune* in 2012. The same year, she was also picked by Mashable as one of the top food writers on Twitter.

Her cookbooks *Modern Spice*, *The Everything Indian Cookbook* and *The Spice Is Right* are as much a feast of tales about food as they are about 'love, life and culture'. Monica recalls being 'over the moon' when top chef Padma Lakshmi picked *Modern Spice* as one of her favourite cookbooks for *Newsweek*. Monica has also fulfilled her dream of writing fiction with her book of short stories, *Devil in Us* where she weaves intricate tales of fate, fortune and love into lessons for life.

When quizzed about how the journey has panned out for her, she laughs and terms it 'battle-scar worthy'. Indeed, every episode that she narrates reveals her never-say-die spirit. Sample this one: In her early writing days, she was at a dinner with a major magazine editor who asked her for her Klout Score, a measure of influence on social media. She had to excuse herself, praying that the washroom had Wi-Fi, to be able to check on the phone what this monster was. Find out she did, and studied it so thoroughly that today she teaches sold-out seminars on the topic.

When asked if success has changed anything for her, the theme of second guessing one's abilities, common to many women achievers raises its head again. she says that even today there are days when she feels that she is 'just an imposter'. Being surrounded by a host of incredible writers 'who have had multiple *New York Times* bestsellers and who are on TV every so often, does make it hard sometimes', she confesses. On the positive side, though she says that the 'high level of insecurity keeps you humble.' A creative pursuit, she admits, is often a 'lonely road with its dark times'. What works for her though each time she hits a writer's block is to learn a new skill. She quotes the Pink Floyd song 'All you touch and all you see, is all your life ever will be.'

What bothers her though are the attempts to box her as an 'Asian–American female writer'. She is quick to point out that she takes tremendous pride in being all three and, in fact, as an Indian writer loves the access to the rich tapestry to draw from. However, predominantly, she wants to be known as someone who informs, inspires and educates rather than being stereotyped and forced to succumb to expectations. Her glass ceiling has been her constant comparison with other writers, primarily the Pulitzer Prize–winning novelist Jhumpa Lahiri. She admits that while undeniably it is a huge honour to be compared to an author of Lahiri's stature, by publishing editors and readers alike, at the end of the day she would prefer to have her own distinctive personality as far as her writing style is concerned.

A distinctive personality she certainly has and one that has won her many admirers. Her biggest fan following is albeit in her own family. Her husband, she confesses, is her sounding board, a shoulder to cry on and someone who pushes her to write on days that are low on productivity. An email about something that he has read or a link to an inspirational book, his ways of keeping her motivated! Her two boys are incredibly proud of what she does; only sometimes she has to go on damage-control mode after a very obvious public display of pride. Turns out, her little one distributed postcards of her latest book in school without her knowledge, for which she had to later send an apology. Her high point, however, was when her mother finally came around to accepting and even feeling proud of her daughter's vocation. The turning point, she thinks, may have come about when articles about her work started to appear in the Indian media and the very people who asked her mother '*Kya matlab hai beti ne naukri chod di?*,' started to gush over the write-ups.

So how does work-life balance work out now in her writing role, I want to know and she regales me first with an account of how terribly out-of-balance life was when both she and her husband were in corporate jobs with unenviable travel schedules. A doctor's visit while wanting to conceive her first child brought things sharply into perspective when she was told that 'part of the deal was that both she and her husband have to be in the same room at the same time'.

Now, she feels blessed to be at a place in life where she can work while her kids are away at school and return to her work later in the night after they have been provided for. She says that she can appreciate this flexibility all the more, having experienced the demands of corporate life. As she puts it, 'It is important that I saw that side but it was not for me.'

Her advice to upcoming writers is, 'Just write. Don't read about writing; don't write about writing. Just write.' She herself begins her day at nine every morning and is a hard taskmaster, as she doesn't let herself go before she has written a minimum of 2000 words. 'The key,' she says, 'is for writers to respect their writing time and not get lost in the noise.' The only other advice she has is, 'Feasts and famines are a part of a freelancer's life; you need to cope with both with equanimity.'

When asked what her advice for other women sitting on the entrepreneurial fence is, she admits that the 'decision is tough as obligations are real'. But then adds, 'The burden of an unfulfilled dream is heavier. If you really want to do it, you will find a way.'

Words that continue to hound me much after the meeting draws to a close.

WORDS OF WISDOM

- 'Do what is important for you. You only get one chance.'
- 'It's not what I do, it's who I am.'
- 'It wasn't a choice. It was a calling.'
- 'If it was right for me, a safety net would appear on its own.'
- 'My attempts at becoming a writer were battle-scar worthy.'
- 'There are days when I feel like an imposter.'
- 'Don't read about writing; don't write about writing, just write.'
- 'The burden of an unfulfilled dream is heavier.'
- 'If you really want to do it, you will find a way.'

Snapshot

Birth sign: Leo

Proudest moment: When my son's teacher told me that he writes well and wants to become like me

Oft-repeated quote: 'All you touch and all you see, is all your life ever will be'—Pink Floyd

Favourite downtime activity: Cooking, painting and colouring with my son

Most inspiring book/author: Vaddey Ratner

One big dream for tomorrow: To finish my novel

Three must-haves for aspiring female entrepreneurs: Confidence, confidence, confidence

SUCHETA PAL

India's first Zumba education specialist and master trainer

Founder:	Just All Heart
Past corporate avatar:	Business Analyst at TCS
Education:	Alumna of Birla Institute of Technology, Mesra
Honours and awards:	The only female ambassador for the Fit India movement supported by the Gujarat government 2015;

	Awarded the Zumba International Brand Ambassador Award 2015, Zumba Pioneer Award 2013 and 2014; First Indian trainer for international celebrity fitness programmes—Piloxing, Insanity, Masala Bhangra Workout and Pound
Just when you thought you had heard it all:	Only Indian to be featured in the Zumba Rush Game 2012 on Xbox Featured on exclusive TV series on Times Zoom TV—'Zumba Dance Fitness Party by Sucheta Pal'

JUST ALL HEART

From overdosing on depression pills in a bid to end her life to earning fame and fortune as the first Indian Zumba master trainer, Sucheta Pal's journey from the depths of despair to the heights of success is one of raw passion and courage. Few know that this powerhouse of energy, credited with bringing about a dance and fitness revolution in India, is an electrical and electronics engineer who started her career as a corporate warrior and left it midway to follow her heart's calling. Persevering in the face of daunting challenges, both monetary and otherwise, to find her true calling in dance, her story is not just an inspiring account of how to live life your way but also a wake-up call for many.

'*You can dance anywhere, even if only in your heart*'—Author unknown

While researching Sucheta's story, I knew that I was preparing myself to meet someone who had had the courage to give up a stable corporate job and follow her heart, and who had then gone on to make a great success out of her choice. No amount of research, however, could have prepared me for this moving account of courage and retribution or for the candid admissions of errors in judgement that led her to a breaking point before the proverbial wake-up call brought about a complete turnaround.

The beginning of her journey is quite uneventful though. The younger daughter of a middle-class household living in small-town Ranchi, her only claim to fame growing up was the fact that she happened to be a junior of Mahendra Singh Dhoni in school. She chuckles as she pronounces it to be 'clearly his loss' that they never dated. Hindi movies constituted a favourite pastime during her growing up years and five-year-old Sucheta found her hero in Aamir Khan while watching his debut movie *Qayamat se Qayamat Tak*. Her laughter fills the room as she describes how anyone who dared to venture into their home could only leave after witnessing a live performance of the famous song, '*Papa Kehte Hain*' by the yet-undiscovered talent, Sucheta. Mithun Chakraborty, the man responsible for bringing the disco revolution to India, however, soon upstaged Aamir Khan in young Sucheta's list of heroes. 'Dancing and singing to Mithun da's signature disco songs was the first time I experienced crazy, unadulterated joy,' she says with a twinkle in her eye. That, in many ways, was the beginning of her dance journey, albeit with a lot of detours in between.

Her parents encouraged both Sucheta and her sister to pursue creative arts, which is why by the time Sucheta turned fifteen, she had already completed training in Indian classical dance besides earning a diploma in fine arts. Creative pursuits apart, her parents were extremely particular that Sucheta secured good grades in school, with the explicit wish of seeing her graduate as a doctor or an engineer. She reflects on the fact that sometimes being a good student can land up being a bane as it 'closes all other doors' for you even if your 'interests happen to lie elsewhere'. The reflections become specific as she recalls how her sister, Pushpita, average in studies and hence not burdened with parental expectations 'did the smart thing', pursuing her interest in fashion designing by enrolling in NIFT. Today she is a successful fashion designer with her own line of leather accessories. It was left to Sucheta, as an exceptional student to adhere to her parent's wishes by taking up a degree in electrical and electronics engineering.

Engineering was followed by a corporate stint as a business analyst. The first couple of years of corporate life went by without a hitch. In fact, she loved the opportunity to travel to different countries on work assignments, Hong Kong being her favourite destination. The move from small-town Ranchi to a bustling metropolis like Mumbai came with a host of lifestyle changes. Finding the culture 'cool' initially, Sucheta became a regular at networking events over drinks and dinner, till it started taking a heavy toll on her body. She was diagnosed with a serious stomach infection, later identified as irritable bowel syndrome (IBS). While still struggling to cope with the ailment, the opportunity to relocate to Hong Kong on a year-long assignment offered the promise of a successful climb up the corporate ladder. Ambitious and eager to make it big, Sucheta was quick to leave for Hong Kong only to return within three months, sick to the point of being physically incapacitated. The illness did not just render her physically weak, it also brought in its wake depression at her physical incapacity to work at par with her peers. Anguish writ large on her face, she describes how depression magnified into social anxiety disorder: 'I was so consumed with fear of people looking down upon me that even attending meetings with four to five people in a room became an impossible task, causing extreme sweating and sometimes even shivering.' The net impact of all this was that she had to move from her business analyst role to performing data-entry jobs that were aimed at reducing her job pressure but did little for her self-esteem. In fact, the move sounded the death knell for someone as ambitious as Sucheta. 'It felt as if my world had come crashing down,' she says, causing her to sink deeper into depression, which in turn only aggravated her IBS. The vicious cycle started playing havoc with her body and mind, so much so that visits to psychiatrists and psychologists became part of her daily grind. The only silver lining during that phase was having the unstinting support of her future husband, then a colleague. Vivek, she recalls, became her anchor during those tough times, driving her to and from therapy sessions and waiting patiently in between.

There is sudden spark in her eye as the conversation steers to her husband. A hard-core techie, he is also a bassist in a rock band, music being their common muse. Married for nearly eight years now, they continue to be the best of friends and cheerleaders for each other.

Coming back to her career, struggling physically and emotionally to cope with this low phase in her life, Sucheta describes how she decided to enrol in a personality development course conducted by an eminent psychologist. While she credits the session with creating a profound impact, the last day of the session ended up shaking her fragile world. She remembers the psychologist asking the participants 'what is that one thing they want to do in life' and her own instinctive reply, 'I want to start a dance school.' It was while working on a business plan for her dream school as part of the course requirement that she started feeling caught between wanting to start a dance school and continuing her corporate job. The dilemma intensified further when towards the end of the session, the psychologist took Sucheta aside to tell her that he saw a lot of potential in her business plan and that she should work towards it. Though encouraging, these words turned toxic for her as she could not muster the courage to take the suggested path. Still in a fragile state of mind, and frustrated by the inability to take control of her life, she decided to end it all by overdosing on depression pills prescribed by her psychiatrist. Her full-throated laugh fills the room as she tells me she learnt that night 'never to try to kill oneself without being sure of the dosage of the pills'. It turns out that the pills were not strong enough to kill her, with the result that Sucheta ended up spending a painful night at home alone, waiting for the elusive death. Come dawn, she mustered just about enough strength to call her sister, who rushed over in panic. Spending two days in the ICU with pipes sticking out of her body brought about the inevitable moment of truth. She confesses then to finally have awoken to a sense of her blessings—a loving family, home, food and all the material comforts, more than what is bestowed upon a vast majority of people in their entire lifetime. Armed with a newfound appreciation for everything in life, she took a vow never to go down the path of self-destruction again.

Once on her feet, Sucheta returned to her corporate job, albeit with the gnawing feeling that something was missing in her life. The breaking point, she recalls, came in a flash when she felt consumed by this overwhelming feeling of being held prisoner while standing in line for food at the office cafeteria. The imagery of food being served out of big buckets, and hundreds of people standing in single file with trays in hand for their share of food conjured up such strong images of a prison camp that she felt an irresistible urge to get out. 'It was as if I was in jail . . . that moment I realized that this was not my life and I wanted to do more. I wanted to do something I felt passionate about,' she says firmly. Putting down her tray, Sucheta simply walked out of the office, certain that she needed to give up this life. With her sister's unconditional words of support—'Do what you want, I am here for you'—ringing in her ears, she gathered the courage to seek temporary absence from work. Not just this, her sister was quick to follow it up with an offer that proved to be a lifesaver for Sucheta, for it gave her the time she needed to figure out the future course of her life. What she was required to do was help her sister run her leather accessory business—a job that necessitated taking a train to the slums of Dharavi every day to supervise the karigars and ensure orders were completed and delivered on time, in return for a monthly allowance of Rs 5000 and accommodation, but most importantly, a chance to follow her dreams.

There is unmistakable pride in her voice as she describes how she gave it her all, waking up at six every morning to catch the early morning train to Dadar to practise jazz, ballet and salsa among other dance forms in Ashley Lobo's Institute for more than four hours. To supplement her meagre earnings, she spent the day selling books to government schools for a paltry 5 per cent sales commission. The day did not end there; evenings were spent at Dharavi, sitting amidst karigars to get orders completed and loaded on to tempos. The last call of the day was to direct the tempo towards the addresses where the delivery had to be made, before heading home at 2–3 a.m. to fall right into bed. Travelling by public buses and trains and surviving on one meal a day consisting mostly of a single vada pav with chai, she recalls how her only concern was not to throw up in the public transport as her stomach was still susceptible to acting up at the slightest provocation. Easily those years gave her the 'most humbling experience' of her life. Being the subject of angry rants from dissatisfied clients, sipping chai with karigars in the stench and heat, travelling by buses in the blistering sun and to top it all, watching nine- to ten-year-olds do full splits with consummate ease while she was trying to get her dance moves right, left 'no space for ego of any kind to thrive'.

While it was a tough schedule to maintain on a daily basis, she says, 'Four hours of uninterrupted dancing in the morning made everything else worthwhile.' 'Dancing,' she reminisces, 'felt magical', the only time she felt whole again, cured of all her physical and emotional ailments.

Dancing brought about a catharsis that was so rejuvenating that she finally decided to give up her corporate life for good and undergo training as a professional dancer, knowing full well that professional dancers earned nowhere near their corporate counterparts, at least not in the short run.

Armed with the knowledge that in dancing lay her true passion, she showed no hesitation in calling it quits; the same courage, however, failed her when it came to telling her parents of this decision. 'It wasn't so much the fear that they would not support me but that I may hurt them with my decision, which kept holding me back. They had spent their life's earnings to make me an engineer and all of sudden I was just giving it up to pursue dance,' she adds, explaining her dilemma. It was only after more than two years of giving up corporate life for dance that she finally mustered up the courage to reveal to her parents that she had indeed said goodbye to the corporate dream. Eyes shining with wisdom learnt the hard way, she says, 'Society has a way of not accepting change till you reach somewhere.' Which is probably why her parents continued to hide the fact that she had quit her job from friends and family, maintaining instead that she was pursuing her love for dance 'on the side'. If I think this could be the source of some bitterness in her, I am proven wrong for she feels nothing but gratitude for their decision to push her into studying engineering, as with hindsight she admits that her qualification stands her in good stead as people tend to take her more seriously.

The one aspect, she admits, that held her in the face of what otherwise could have been crippling fear, is the 'solid support system' comprising of her sister and her fiancé. Little surprise then, that her advice to all aspiring entrepreneurs is, 'Ensure that you have someone who will back you up in case you stumble so that you can land on your two feet.'

Tying the knot in 2008 and settling into a new routine, her world was again shaken up when Vivek announced that he would need to temporarily relocate to the US on a client assignment. Unwilling to let go of her professional dance training, but being a self-confessed 'sucker for love' she ended up accompanying him to the US, albeit reluctantly. Determined to continue her dance training in the US, she chanced upon Zumba while surfing for dance studios. Wondering what kind of African dance constituted Zumba, Sucheta was nevertheless impressed enough by the studio pictures, to set out to have a look at it. She recalls trudging half a mile in knee-deep snow to reach the dance studio. 'Opening the doors of the studio was like opening the floodgates to a whole new world,' she says. Stepping inside, her eyes fell upon this huge colourful place filled with eighty people eagerly waiting for the class to begin. Instinctively, she took her place in the last row, all the while wondering what prompted so many people to come out in a blistering snowstorm for an African dance, only to realize a little later that she was witnessing a worldwide fitness phenomenon.

The next couple of minutes are etched in her memory forever, for they changed her life permanently. She remembers tears streaming down her face listening to the music, put on by the instructor, an obese lady with a beatific smile on her face. Memories of the gay abandon and unadulterated joy she had experienced while dancing to Mithun's songs as a child or even the crazy joyous dance that accompanies every Ganpati Visarjan in Mumbai came flooding and the fact that eighty people could have fun while working out had Sucheta hooked from the moment go. Zumba became her life for the next six months. She became a regular client of the studio, taking back-to-back morning and evening classes and loving every part of it. Her dedication was rewarded when, impressed with her dancing skills, the owner of the studio offered Sucheta the job of a Zumba instructor. Just as I marvel at her ability to give it her all, comes an honest admission that her first class as an instructor was a fiasco; within the first five minutes six people had walked out and the next thirty minutes saw the class size reduce by half. When asked if it demoralized her, she admits that on the contrary, it brought about the realization that knowing Zumba is very different from taking a Zumba class. With an appreciation for the high standards that Americans hold everyone up to, she vowed never to underestimate her students or overestimate her own capabilities. With her never-say-die spirit, she admits that thankfully the 'team did not give up on her after the disastrous first class'. With their support and encouragement and of course her own tireless efforts, a month later, she was declared the top trainer at the studio. It is worth a mention that the very studio went on to be declared the best dance studio in Connecticut three times in a row. Very soon, her Zumba events were packed to capacity and Sucheta was making quite a name for herself among the community of Zumba instructors.

The big break came in 2012 when the founder of Zumba, Alberto Perlman, came visiting her town. Impressed by her credentials, he encouraged her to participate in the auditions for Zumba master trainer to be held in Miami, later in the year. Her first reaction was a resounding no, as all the demons of the past came back to haunt her. She remembers telling her husband, 'How can I go for the auditions as I will not be able to utter a single word in front of so many people.' Gratitude fills her voice as she recounts how he motivated her, reminding her of her remarkable strength in turning her life around from the verge of breakdown to teaching dance to a packed class of foreign nationals. His words—'If you can get to this point, you can certainly go further'—gave her the push needed to sign up for the Zumba master trainer auditions.

They moved to Miami for a month and Sucheta sailed through her audition and training process to emerge as the first Indian Zumba master trainer and education specialist. 'It was a sublime feeling, holding the title in my hand. I felt like I had conquered the world,' she recalls.

Sucheta felt remarkably confident about the future after acquiring her Zumba master trainer certificate and prepared to return to India, although her husband was still in the US working on his project. With her trademark grin, she tells me how little she knew of what lay in store for her back in her homeland.

A few days were enough to drive home the point that Zumba was still an unknown name in India, except in very niche pockets. I get a sense of the difficulties she must have encountered, as she goes on to recount her very first Zumba trainer class in India. Prior to Sucheta's return, Zumba sessions in India were conducted by international trainers sent specially for the purpose by the Zumba head office in Miami. While Sucheta was packing her bags for her flight home, a Zumba session to be held in Pune by Anna, a Romanian Zumba master trainer, ran into difficulties. Anna was not able to get a visa in time to travel and the Zumba office, not able to arrange anyone else to fly in at such short notice, requested her to fill in. While the session itself turned out to be a huge success, an altercation before the start of the session taught her some important lessons.

Enquiring about a ruckus at the counter before the start of her session, she was informed that a lady was demanding a refund. Stepping in to speak to her, the lady was blunt enough to tell her that she had enrolled for the session because 'a foreign trainer' was visiting. Since Anna could not make it, she did not want to attend the session and hence wanted a refund. Sucheta's explanation that all Zumba master trainers receive the same training failed to placate the lady who continued to demand her money back. Extremely angry now at this prejudice against her own kin, she ended up telling the lady to take her refund and return only when she had more faith in fellow Indians. The lady left with her money but Sucheta's vindication came when the same lady returned a year later to learn Zumba from a 'fellow Indian'.

Since then Sucheta has made it her mission to take Zumba to every street and corner of India. It has been virtually a road trip for the last three years, with not a single weekend spent at home. Not that she is complaining as it has given her an opportunity to indulge in her twin passions—travelling and dancing. Today there are umpteen Zumba sessions packed to capacity happening simultaneously across the country, all thanks to the zeal and drive of this one lady who dreamt of making Zumba a household name. To her goes the credit of having trained more than 2500 trainers in India within the last three years alone, no mean feat.

Her biggest success perhaps is the way her parents now support her efforts wholeheartedly and feel a sense of pride watching her TV shows and interviews. The staunchest advocate of her craft, however, is her mother-in-law, who, at sixty-five years of age and suffering from arthritis, has the drive to stand in the first row of her sessions and learn Zumba along with the younger lot. With a hard-to-miss resolve, Sucheta holds up her mother-in-law as a model student to anyone who complains of not being able to keep up with their fitness regime.

When asked if entrepreneurship has taught her any important lessons that she would like to share with other wannabe entrepreneurs, she points out that early on in her entrepreneurial journey she realized that she 'could either chase passion or money, but could not conceivably chase both'. She chose passion and tells other entrepreneurs to do likewise for she firmly believes, 'If you chase your passion, money will eventually follow.' She is quick to add a word of caution though, 'You need to be sure about what you want to do.' 'Take your own litmus tests before taking the leap,' she recommends, the parallel to the times when she took a sabbatical to find her calling, unmistakable.

The one other advice she has for women professionals is to stand up for their rights. 'What bothers me is that women don't fight enough for what they deserve, preferring to be cast in the good-girl mould that society prefers to see them in. We are expected to be nice to our in-laws, spend time with family, send kids to school on time, but never ask for our fair share. This needs to change,' she says. In her own professional life she has experienced the biases where male show organizers have thought that being a woman performer they could cow her. She admits that each time it has happened, she has risen up and made her point of view known. She laughs her full-throated laugh as she points out that men tend to take their sense of entitlement very seriously, whether it is the professional sphere or something as offensive as sticking their elbows out of their seats while on aeroplanes, not realizing how inconvenient it can be for the lady sitting next to them. With so much travel on her plate, she has ensured that she makes her annoyance at the jutting elbows known.

When asked what has been the most gratifying part of her journey, she admits that it is the lives she has touched and often changed. There is no mistaking the pride in her eyes as she recalls a moving letter she received from Sandra, a Zumba trainer trained by her. A cancer survivor, she writes regularly to Sucheta to let her know that training under her gave new meaning and direction to her life. Then there is this lady who had never stepped out of her small home town, Shillong, but found it in her, to come all the way to Delhi to train under Sucheta, giving her life a whole new purpose. There are many more such stories, each one of them mirroring in some way Sucheta's own sojourn of overcoming limiting beliefs to follow that one crazy passion that gives meaning and substance to life.

WORDS OF WISDOM

- 'It was as if I was in jail . . . that moment I realized that wasn't my life and I wanted to do more. I wanted to do something I felt passionate about.'
- 'Four hours of uninterrupted dancing in the morning made everything else worthwhile.'
- '[Ensure] you have someone who will back you up in case you stumble so that you can land on your two feet.'
- 'Society has a way of not accepting change till you reach somewhere.'
- 'Be sure about what you want to do. Take your own litmus tests before taking the leap.'
- '[Early on in my entrepreneurial journey] I realized that I could either chase passion or money, but could not conceivably chase both. If you chase your passion, money will eventually follow.'
- 'We are expected to be nice to our in-laws, spend time with family, send kids to school on time, but never ask for our fair share. This needs to change.'

Snapshot

Birth sign: Libra

Biggest role model: An eighty-five-year-old lady who I met at a convention in Florida, who, despite being physically incapacitated, was dancing in the front row. Have met many such role models since.

Proudest moment: Being awarded three years in a row by Zumba Fitness—Zumba Pioneer Award in 2013 and 2014 and Zumba Ambassador Award in 2015.

Oft-repeated quote: 'Just all heart'

Favourite downtime activity: Dancing

One big dream for tomorrow: Basic amenities in the form of clean restrooms in cities and on highways to ensure hygiene and safety for women

Three must-haves for aspiring female entrepreneurs: Focus on one thing at a time; never forget the people who were with you when you were a nobody; take care of your health and your self-worth.

KANIKA TEKRIWAL

Entrepreneur
Co-founder and CEO, JetSetGo Aviation Services Pvt. Ltd

Co-Founder and CEO: JetSetGo Aviation Services Pvt. Ltd
Past Corporate Avatar: Indiabulls and Aerospace Resources
Education: Alumna of Coventry University
Honours and Awards: Featured among 30 global women entrepreneurs under 30 by BBC;

	Listed as one of the 100 most inspirational women in the world, 2015 by BBC
Just when you thought you had heard it all:	Marathon runner, painter, avid traveller

GIVING WINGS TO HER DREAMS

When you hail from a conservative Marwari family from small-town Bhopal, your life is pretty much laid out for you. Marriage by the age of twenty-three, children by twenty-five and you are thereafter expected to devote the rest of your life taking care of the home and hearth. This is exactly what Kanika Tekriwal grew up hearing throughout her impressionable years. Nothing, however, could rein in her spirit. Determined to follow her dreams, she began by pursuing a corporate career, wanting to eventually turn to entrepreneurship—till fate intervened in the form of a dreaded disease!

Defying the doctor's prognosis, she managed to rid her body of cancer cells, in the process emerging stronger and more determined than ever to achieve her entrepreneurial dreams. Today her venture JetSetGo, popularly referred to as the Uber of the skies, is redefining aviation. Hailed as one of the 100 most inspirational women of the world by a BBC Survey, 2015, hers is a heart-warming story of the relentless pursuit of hope!

'Your wings already exist, all you have to do is fly'—Author unknown

Even before I met Kanika, I had seen her smiling face show up on the many links that were all over social media. It was with a lot of anticipation, therefore, that I set out to discover what lay beneath the surface of this woman who counts her brush with cancer as a blessing in disguise, save her as it did from the burden of parental expectations revolving around marriage. A few minutes into our meeting and there is no doubt that here is a woman who has beaten every cliché to the ground. In the process, she has managed to quietly change the face of Indian aviation forever, that too at an age where most others are still trying to figure out their goal in life.

Born into a conservative family in a quiet town like Bhopal does not provide much fodder for excitement, which is why her childhood years, she explains, went by uneventfully. Her one big memory revolves around watching a helicopter landing, with the big round eyes of a stupefied four-year-old. Not knowing what to think, she started crying, assuming that a giant cockroach had made its way there. The pilots were quick to reassure her and even offered to give her a guided tour of the helicopter in an effort to cheer her up. This innocuous tryst perhaps sparked off a lifelong obsession with the blue skies. She recalls how through her growing up years, she wanted to be a pilot; a dream that was effectively squashed by her father when he made it clear that this was not a profession befitting girls of their family.

Life took a turn when she entered boarding school in Ooty as a fourth-grade student. This was Kanika's first encounter with life beyond the four walls of the house and she found herself opening up fast to a world of possibilities. As she puts it, 'Boarding school provided me the opportunity to think, dream and look beyond books.' Boarding school was followed by a bachelor's degree in art and fashion technology in Mumbai, again with a view to widening her horizon.

At home, however, marriage remained the sole topic of discussion, as she faced the inevitable prospect of being married off immediately after completing her studies. There is a world of amusement in her voice as she recalls how even birthday presents from her parents almost always constituted jewellery, as a build-up to her bridal trousseau.

Knowing in her heart that she wanted to pursue her dreams, she had by then learnt to keep her thoughts to herself so as to maintain peace at home. The first time she verbalized her dreams to someone was aboard an aeroplane. Kanika vividly remembers taking this flight from Mumbai to Bhopal as a fourteen-year-old and being literally forced into a conversation by a very persistent co-passenger. She found herself strangely opening up to his innocent question on 'what do you want to do' and while disclosing her dreams ended up telling him, 'I don't think any of them will materialize because of the way things work in my family. Also because everyone thinks my ideas are stupid.' His subsequent lines have remained an inspiration to her forever. Quoting the famous saying 'First they ignore you, then they laugh at you, then they fight you, then you win,' he advised her to keep faith in herself and never give up even when the whole world was against her. Advice that has stood her in good stead in later life!

Cognizant of the fact that working post-marriage would hinge on the whims of her husband's family, Kanika decided to make the most of time available with her, after her graduation, to gain work experience. She was clearly pushing the envelope as no one in her extended family had ever held a corporate job and ended up working as an assistant vice president with Indiabulls, which, as luck would have it, after opening an aviation arm, which gave Kanika the perfect brush with her dreams.

Keen to expand her horizons further, her corporate stint was followed by an MBA from Coventry University in the UK. She recalls how her MBA once again brought to the fore a clash between her desires and family expectations. Wanting to major in marketing, she had to take up finance because as her father put it, 'Marketing will involve meeting outsiders, which your would-be in laws might not like.' Finance was considered to be a safer option because that would not involve meeting anyone outside and odds were that her in-laws 'could let her work in this field'.

While she had to buy this logic, her heart clearly lay elsewhere. It was while in the UK that she once again turned to the corporate sector, working not in finance but in the highly people-driven field of business development, with aerospace and aviation consultants Aerospace Resources. While she thoroughly enjoyed her job, what it also gave her besides financial independence were ample opportunities to work in close association with air charter companies in India, which was to work to her advantage later in life.

Management degree earned, it was time to bid adieu to her thriving corporate career and return to India. When asked if there was an element of fear in this homecoming as it could well signal the end of her independent lifestyle and perhaps also the end of her working life, you get a sense of determination that defines Kanika. She admits that while she was bidding adieu to a corporate career, she did it without many qualms, as in her heart she knew that this was not the end of the road. 'Despite all this talk about settling down I always had this conviction that one day I would start my own business; only when and how I didn't know.' There's laughter in her voice as she jokes, 'If nothing else I thought I would design clothes as that could find favour with prospective in-laws.'

She recalls how while heading to India her plan was to start her own enterprise based in the National Capital Region. Though she did not know what exactly she would be doing, the blueprint of JetSetGo, her aviation venture to be launched later in life, was already brewing in her head. Coming from a corporate set-up, where everything was institutionalized, didn't the uncertainty of beginning from scratch scare her, I ask. With a disarming smile she confesses that while there were the normal fears that accompany any change, the likelihood of being able to build something on her own seemed pregnant with possibilities. Not discounting the fact that finance is an important constituent of a start-up, she recalls how, even at this stage, she instinctively knew that if she remained true to her passion, money would follow.

Before she embarked on her entrepreneurial journey, however, her parents convinced her to come home to Bhopal for at least fifteen days with the promise of paying serious attention to her business plans. It is at this time that fate intervened to upturn all their plans.

She remembers visiting the doctor for a nagging pain in her arm, all the while preparing herself mentally for the line-up of boys that her parents had arranged for her to meet in the hope of getting her married off within the year. The doctor, a family friend, was unable to figure out the source of pain but suggested the name of a clinic for further testing without giving away any signs of his medical suspicions. She recalls how the diagnosis of non-Hodgkin's lymphoma, a cancer that affects the lymphatic system, caught her completely off guard. From there began her journey of rediscovery, strength and resilience in the face of overwhelming odds.

I get a glimpse into her never-say-die attitude as she describes her brush with cancer. 'The first doctor I met told me you have very little time. I was twenty-two at that time and I said, I am going to come and see you here after forty years, not for treatment, but to prove that I am alive and kicking,' she says with determination. The journey to battle cancer took her to the doorsteps of numerous doctors till she eventually found one whom she could trust completely and who in turn had faith in her ability to survive the deadly disease. The search for the right doctor, she explains, ended up teaching her an important life lesson: 'The first major lesson I learned here was that choosing your people right is very important; keep looking till you find them, and believe in them completely.' Cancer, she believes, has moulded her into the person she is today. In her own words, 'Cancer made me a strong person ready to face any challenge; and most importantly, to never give in. So when we began work on JetSetGo and things didn't go my way I didn't get upset, but just focused on what we could do next.'

She regards cancer as a blessing for not only did it give her the much needed reprieve from parental pressure, it also gave her time to introspect and give shape to her business plans. As she describes it, 'Cancer happened and everything else fell aside. It gave me time to think of a lot of stuff and, most importantly, it gave me a lot of courage.'

Nine months into her fight against cancer, and numerous chemotherapies later, she got a clean chit from her doctor. The memory of that day remains fresh in her mind. 'The day I recovered, I packed my bags and moved to Delhi because I knew that sitting in Bhopal, I was not going to be able to do anything.' Plus, there was this burning desire to get away from well-meaning relatives who mourned her lack of marriageability as a survivor of a deadly disease.

The move to Delhi, she confesses, was not easy. It led to temporary estrangement between father and daughter as her father wanted her to stay back for at least another year in order to convalesce from the ailment. Kanika, however, had made up her mind and there was no stopping her. 'I didn't want to feel sorry for myself any longer. I would have needed a shrink if I stayed home doing nothing,' she says. She remembers her father being so angry that many months passed before he picked up the phone to speak to her.

She admits, though, that she had no idea how she would go about setting up her business in Delhi. One thing was clear; she was not going to return to a corporate job. Cancer had built up these blocks in her head. 'After nine months of being away from a job and with a disease like cancer, I thought I had become unemployable,' she says. Musing back to the early days of her shift to Delhi, she says, 'I had built JetSetGo completely in my brain. Now how to get it started was the big question.' She found her answer in starting a consultancy service, which made sure that she was 'involved with every operator possible, every aircraft owner and every passenger to figure out if they really needed JetSetGo'. With two other business partners, one of them based in Europe and the other in the US, her consultancy helped airlines and operators sell aircrafts, optimize operations, marketing and revenue. More importantly, consulting gave her an opportunity to enter any operator's office and understand the market potential for her business. That aside, it helped pay the bills and also make enough to live on for almost two years.

Setting out to execute her plan after testing the market sufficiently, the initial phase, she recalls, was tough. She makes no bones about the fact that she was laughed at and ridiculed openly. With a laptop in her hand she remembers making the rounds of every supplier till one in particular decided to be openly critical. As he ruthlessly mocked at her naiveté in assuming that people would book jet planes online, Kanika recalls going home and howling the night away. With self-doubt creeping in, 'I kept thinking, maybe it won't work, maybe no one will support me.' However, nothing, least of all naysayers, could keep her down and out for too long, as she was determined to give wings to her dreams.

Amidst the many congratulatory messages that came her way after she set up JetSetGo successfully, the one message that she particularly holds dear is a text message that she received from the same supplier that read 'Only you could have grown JetSetGo into what it is today'. She confesses how she read the message 'probably fifteen times'. 'I wanted to jump. If I could fly, I would have flown; it felt so good.' More than the message itself, it was the feeling of being finally accepted by the same group of people who refused to give credence to her idea earlier that gives her the greatest satisfaction. 'I have not even achieved 2 per cent of what I want to achieve, but they are all coming around,' she adds.

There are many instances of her encountering the proverbial glass ceiling in the highly patriarchal world of aviation, but nothing deterred Kanika from moving towards the goal she had set for herself. Sample this: 'One day, I walked into a meeting slightly late. Somebody from the client's team asked me if I could order some coffee thinking I was the secretary.' She smiles as she confesses that in the beginning such instances could rattle her up, but now she not only takes them in her stride but also finds humour in it.

When asked about her first round of funding, she has an interesting tale to tell. Driven by the firm belief, 'Brilliant businesses are not built on money alone but on great people and great ideas,' she says, 'I was keen to strike the right partnership to associate with my brand.' It was while reading about YouWeCan Ventures in one of the business magazines that the obvious synergies of working with an enterprise backed by a personality like Yuvraj Singh struck her. She managed to get in touch with some of his colleagues who put her in touch with his fund manager. 'A fifty-minute phone conversation sealed the funding for us,' she explains. She recalls how strong YouWeCan's conviction was in the product that even before she could come to terms with the fact, she was advised to send not a term sheet, but a shareholder's agreement. Point out the similarity in the fact that both she and Yuvraj have fought and emerged stronger from the dreaded C disease and Kanika tells how Yuvraj Singh and the fund weren't aware about her having suffered from cancer when they signed up. She recalls a conversation that she and Yuvraj had on affordable healthcare (months after the investment was closed), where she happened to mention how unaffordable 'PET scans' are. Extremely surprised about her being aware of PET scans in the first place, he asked her how she knew of their unaffordability. That is when they connected over a shared ordeal.

Today Kanika has a long list of achievements to her name. JetSetGo has emerged as the first-of-its-kind private jet concierge service that works like an online marketplace making jets available to passengers. Her company also works in the area of medical evacuation, air ambulances and helicopter arrangements. Being featured in BBC's list of thirty under-30 young women entrepreneurs and then again in its list of 100 most inspirational women in the world, one of only seven Indians in the list, has brought her achievements to the forefront. When asked about the experience of being included in this roll of honour, she says, 'It was like a heart attack to see my name on the list, it was a real shock.' She then elaborates, 'BBC called and wanted to interview me for thirty under-30 women entrepreneurs, which I thought is fine, as there may not be so many women entrepreneurs under thirty, so maybe they got my name in there.' The next thing she knew she was reading a message left by a member of her extended family that they had also seen her on the 100 inspirational women list. She recalls clicking on the link enclosed in the message to find her face staring back at her from among a list of illustrious women. Congratulatory messages have not stopped pouring in since then from friends, family and the industry.

When quizzed on her greatest entrepreneurial learning in her journey, she admits that perseverance is the biggest weapon to conquer all the vicissitudes of being an entrepreneur. 'You might be the best planner in the world but your day will never go according to your plan. Tears, blood, sweat are all part of the game; no one said it was going to be easy,' she says.

Her advice for women sitting on the entrepreneurial fence is, 'If you believe in yourself you can do it. You have to conquer your fears yourself; nobody else can do it for you. You can't know unless you try.'

Like most entrepreneurs, work-life balance remains her biggest challenge. She laughs when she says, 'Forget balance, there is no life for now, it is all about work and more work.' Not that she is complaining! There is no missing the humorous glint in her eye as she cites a real-life example of how she has not had time to get the light at her house fixed, which is why she had been forced to live in darkness at home for the last few days. A marathon runner, her running has been lately reduced to jogging along the hallways of her building to clear her head after returning from office, often during the wee hours of the morning.

As I get ready to bid this powerhouse of energy and optimism adieu, I cannot but help asking her of her marriage plans, a tape that has run throughout her life. 'Marriage can wait, my dreams can't,' she says. She relates how her family now stands firmly behind her, finally leaving the decision of marriage to her.

From having been written off from life itself, Kanika is today the poster girl for women and their right to follow their dreams. Hers has been a remarkable journey with many twists and turns, but more importantly, one that she has steered by the dint of her unstinting belief in herself. She is modest about her achievements, though, as she mentions that she has a long way to go. 'When I really make a change in the aviation industry, when investors start perceiving the aviation sector as a profitable investment, then I will feel I have achieved something.'

As I walk out of her office, there is palpable positivity and optimism in the air.

WORDS OF WISDOM

- 'The first doctor I met told me you have very little time. I was twenty-two at that time and I said, I am going to come and see you here after forty years, not for treatment, but to prove that I am alive and kicking.'
- 'Cancer made me a strong person ready to face any challenge; and most importantly, to never give in. So when we began work on JetSetGo and things didn't go my way—I didn't get upset, but just focused on what we could do next.'
- 'Cancer was the most emotionally draining episode of my life, but you know what, it helped me become a better person, a successful person and most importantly, a stronger person.'
- 'The first major lesson I learned here was that choosing your people right is very important; keep looking till you find them, and believe in them completely.'
- 'Brilliant businesses were not built on money alone, but on great people and great ideas.'
- 'It takes a lot of perseverance to be an entrepreneur. You might be the best planner in the world but your day will never go according to your plan.'
- 'If you believe in yourself you can do it. You have to conquer your fears yourself; nobody else can do it for you. You can't know unless you try.'
- 'Tears, blood, sweat are all part of the game; no one said it was going to be easy.'
- 'I have a long way to go; when I really make a change in the aviation industry, when investors start perceiving the aviation sector as a profitable investment, then I will feel I have achieved something.'

Snapshot

Birth sign: Gemini

Biggest role model: Richard Branson

Proudest moment: When a customer came and told me that he wanted to invest in my company

Oft-repeated quote: 'Don't take no for an answer.'

Favourite downtime activity: Running. I have run the Delhi Half Marathon and have also trekked the Himalayas.

Most inspiring book/author: The autobiography of Richard Branson

One big dream for tomorrow: To revolutionize private aviation

Three must-haves for aspiring female entrepreneurs: Perseverance, patience, fearlessness

ABHA MARYADA BANERJEE

India's first female motivational speaker, Author

Founder:	Success India Leadership Company
Past corporate avatar:	Lawyer/Activist
Education:	Alumna of Delhi University, Faculty of Law
Honours and awards:	Rex Karma Veer Chakra Award 2014 by the United Nations and International Confederation of NGOs

Author:	*Nucleus: Power Women Lead from the Core* *Maryada—In Rendition*
Just when you thought you had heard it all:	Peak Performance and Mental Strength Coach for Indian Olympic Athletes, 2012; Hailed as the Asian Oprah Winfrey

VOICE OF CHANGE

How often do you meet a woman who, at the age of thirty-five, decides to give up a decade-long legal career to take a leap of faith, that too with a six-year-old son in tow? But then, how many women you know are on a mission to change the world?

From being called 'mentally retarded' for giving up the luxuries of a settled life to being regarded as one of the leading life, business and success coaches in the Asia-Pacific, Abha's journey has indeed been spectacular. It has seen her metamorphose from a woman in search of her true identity into someone who uses her remarkable motivational powers to influence others into believing in their own worth. This is her journey of change.

'A leader is one who knows the way, goes the way, and shows the way'—John Maxwell, author and leadership expert

A *woman with a purpose* is what springs instinctively to mind as I meet Abha, whose children, she confesses, have christened her 'live entertainment' and beg her to 'sit still for a few minutes'. Speak to her for some time and the one aspect of her persona that shines through is her palpable will to bring about social change.

The eldest of three daughters, Abha, recalls how she was expected to lead her sisters by example. She, however, had other plans, and none of them included playing with dolls. More interested in leading mohalla morchas in favour of stray animals than playing with her sisters at home, much of her early life was spent rebelling against popular ideas about how a girl should behave. Abha found herself more often than not at the receiving end of reprimands, the moniker 'troublemaker' sticking with her through her growing-up years.

She recalls how her father, a lawyer himself, worried about the future of his extremely idealistic daughter, suggested law as a career to fight injustice. The idea struck root and Abha enrolled in law college to come out four years later as a qualified barrister ready to take up the cause of the less privileged. However, practising law for ten years left Abha thoroughly disillusioned and restless. In her own words, 'Law challenged my conscience every day as what the law books claim does not exist in the real world.' The dichotomy struck hard at her conscience; while the poor who needed representation could not afford the services of a lawyer, the rich could buy dozens of lawyers to suppress an already suppressed group of people.

There was also the added aspect of being a woman in a male dominated set-up and Abha often found herself at the receiving end of the prevailing bias, getting bypassed for increments and promotions. Her father had instilled the virtues of hard work in all his children, but Abha soon discovered that it held no merit in the sycophantic, politics-ridden world of business and law. She did not believe in exchanging social favours or networking beyond office hours just to get a leg up the corporate ladder; so colleagues with much less experience, skill and output ended up getting salary raises and promotions while she continued to be stuck in the same position. Thoroughly disillusioned with the profession of law, she decided to call it quits though the fighter in her was not satisfied till the company had cleared all her dues in full.

This was neither the first nor the only time Abha was forced to encounter the challenges of being a woman in a male bastion. Disdain writ large on her face, she recounts how she was often subject to sexist remarks, especially when trying to raise funds for her business venture. Justifiably proud of the fact that there have been no compromises and shortcuts en route to success, she urges all women to avoid the lure of resorting to the easy way in the hope of reaching their dreams sooner, only to end up bitterly regretting it later.

Thoroughly disappointed by the business of law and the impact that it could make but did not, Abha, on the advice of some friends, even dabbled in politics briefly with the intent to create social impact. She, however, ended up being even more disappointed, with the hypocrisy at the heart of political manoeuvres. The exit from politics was as quick as the entry.

She believes it was destiny that took her on the path of personal development. Drawn to the teachings of Swami Vivekananda from a very young age, Abha read ancient scriptures and was mesmerized by how they emphasized that every individual had the power to control life events by simply shifting the thought process. Intrigued, she turned to the Internet to research the nascent personal development industry. With a definitive sense of right and wrong and the desire to bring about change, she immediately knew this was where she had to be.

At the age of thirty-five and with a young child who needed attention, she recalls how her decision to quit law and return to studying personal development invited criticism from her near and dear ones. Nothing, not even the barrage of criticism that came her way, could deter Abha. From being labelled 'mentally retarded' by her own family to being called 'overambitious', the onslaught left her undaunted and at times even amused. Not only was she changing her career midstream, she was doing it for something as esoteric as motivational speaking, which made her the butt of jokes among family and friends. Not one to mince words, she confesses, 'I have been called stupid, *hawabaaz*, arrogant, psychopath, megalomanic, narcissistic, and a lot more.'

When asked if the thought of giving up ever crossed her mind, you get a hint of the iron resolve that has helped her reach where she is today. 'It was something I never considered,' she says. 'I never had a plan B. Plan A had to succeed and I did whatever I could humanly see, think and imagine,' she adds.

The fact that the personal development industry was still at a very nascent stage in India around the turn of the millennium meant limited opportunities to learn and grow. Not one to give up easily, she continued to explore and eventually chanced upon Singapore, nearer home with its many learning opportunities in the form of personal development courses and self-study material. Her very first trip to Singapore, however, ended up costing a fortune and Abha found herself hitting another roadblock. Extended stays in Singapore, something she needed in order to gain mastery over the subject, she realized were going to be costly and not feasible in the now single-income household. The problem looked insurmountable till her husband suggested that they consider shifting out of India.

As the conversation steers to her husband, Abha has a smile playing on her lips as she recalls that as a short, thin girl with average looks, her parents had a difficult time finding a suitable match for her. Determined to marry without dowry, Abha did not make the search any easier, not to mention that her fiery responses sent many a prospective groom scooting. Marry she eventually did, but on her own terms and to a groom who respected her as an equal. Batchmates at law school, it took her future husband more than three years to convince Abha to say yes to his proposal. Twenty-three years later, with two great additions to the family, the foundation is even deeper, each cheering the other on to greater success.

Circling back to her career, the family shifted base to Indonesia, which turned out to be perfect in all respects. Close to Singapore, it made travelling frequently to attend the plethora of courses manageable. Of course, this is not to suggest that the transition to studies was easy. When asked if fear had any place in this phase, she tells a tale of meticulous planning. 'I took great pains to ensure that I was fully prepared financially before taking this leap of faith. I cleared all outstanding debts and was extremely particular about keeping expenses low as long as I was not adding to the family income.' With no pressure of monthly instalments, she managed to keep a tight leash on household expenses and used her savings to fund her learning. There is a wealth of wisdom in her words as she equates those years of struggle to living the 'life of a fakir, trying not to spend the money

I did not make as yet. It taught me a lesson in frugality, contentment and delayed gratification. There was no place for regret or guilt as it was part of a massive journey and I enjoyed it all.' It is a testament to Abha's dedication and commitment that over the years, she ended up taking more than sixty-five courses and reading thousands of books on self-development, coaching and motivation before taking the plunge towards active mentoring and coaching.

Little surprise then that her advice to all women looking to take the plunge into entrepreneurship is to have complete control over their mental, emotional and financial space. Her poetic recommendation sums it all:

'Do what it takes . . .
Then just JUMP and enjoy FLYING'

It took Abha more than five years to get her first taste of being accepted in the personal development space. The breakthrough came in 2006 when some common acquaintances, impressed with her skills, suggested her name for a conference on motivation being held in Singapore. She remembers the butterflies in her stomach as she was called on stage. An impulsive decision to go extempore leaving the script behind proved to be a great judgement call as it endeared the audience to her honesty of purpose, her simplicity and her relatable vulnerability. Since then, every motivational talk has been impromptu; she finds a script limiting, preferring a freewheeling discussion to explore and engage with the audience. With an array of techniques—from poetry to street theatre, active monologue to role plays—her motivational speeches have always succeeded in creating a lasting impact on her audience.

Today, she is hailed not just as India's first woman motivational speaker but is fondly called the Asian Oprah and has a number of other feathers in her cap, including working with Indian athletes for the 2012 Olympics as their Peak Performance and Mental Strength Coach. She particularly recalls coaching boxer Usha Nagisetty, a two-time World Championship silver medallist. Having undergone a knee surgery, Usha was going through a phase of depression and serious lack of self-belief. The fact that as her Mental Strength Coach, Abha succeeded in getting her to once again don the boxing gloves and return to the arena with a renewed confidence remains one of the most gratifying milestones of Abha's journey.

The journey to success has been long; when asked whether, typical of all entrepreneurs, she ever struggled with self-doubt, her response is: 'I was convinced that rejection means nothing more than someone not being able to see what you see.' You know that she isn't mouthing a cliché, when she regales you with an incident that once again speaks of her sheer willpower.

This was when she had enrolled for a media course in India with the objective of learning how to convert her speeches into visual medium for greater reach and impact. As a girl with average looks, when she asked the course director to teach her the tricks of standing in front of the camera, he was rude enough to remark that with her looks, anchoring was not for her and a role behind the camera might be more appropriate. She kept requesting and the director kept resisting in the same mode till one day, Abha let him know in no uncertain terms that she intended to learn the tricks of standing in front of the camera and not behind and it would be best for him to get on with his job of teaching her the same. He agreed reluctantly and was forced to eat his words when Abha, with her usual focus and determination, ended up being presented the best student prize by the same course director.

I get a glimpse of her multifaceted talent when she tells me that in between her speaking and coaching assignments, she was lucky enough to get an opportunity to participate in a gathering of Hindi poets, which opened the doors to a literary career. Attended by heavyweights of the Hindi poetic world such as Javed Akhtar, Abha decided to pen a few poems herself to recite on the occasion. Encouraged by how well her poems were received, she decided to compile them into a book. Derived out of her own middle name, Maryada, which means maintaining one's honour, the book is both a tribute to Hindi literature and a testimony to her own strength of purpose.

Her next book, *Nucleus*, has brought her worldwide fame and recognition, earning her the distinction of being listed among the top influencers of the world. The inspiration for the book came to her while attending a conference in Jakarta where the gender friction in the room came out in to the open when one of the participants asked her how she could 'talk so confidently about global practices being a woman from India'. Abha devoted the next few months synthesizing her own experience and education into defining a ten-step methodology to help women break out of the daily rut and lead successful lives. 'The sheer experience of holding my book for the first time cannot be explained in words,' she says. With her daughter and husband happily doing a victory dance, she herself could only fight back tears holding a book bearing her name and picture on the cover, for she had poured herself mentally and emotionally into its content.

No amount of accolades or awards, however, can change a person as firmly rooted as Abha. I can see it in the way she tells me how her children can bring her back to earth simply by remarking that her 'cooking failed to meet the mark today or that my clothes are not in their usual place'. Home and hearth define her as much as her work and she ensures that she invests in both.

A firm supporter of women power, her advice to women sitting on the entrepreneurial fence is that they can achieve anything provided they learn to get past their own self-doubts. As a coach, she has seen many intelligent women guilt-ridden and filled with doubts regarding their ability to achieve their goals, and her first action is always to remind them to take it one step at a time. For that is how Abha's journey to success began, one slow step at a time.

WORDS OF WISDOM

- 'Rejection means nothing more than someone not being able to see what you see.'
- 'Law challenged my conscience every day, it pained me to read the books that meant nothing in real life as soon as you shut them.'
- 'I took great pains to ensure that I was fully prepared financially before taking this leap of faith.'
- 'Do what it takes . . . Then just jump and enjoy flying.'
- 'I never had a plan B. Plan A had to succeed and I did whatever I could humanly see, think and imagine.'
- 'Take it one step at a time.'

Snapshot

Birth sign: Aquarius

Biggest role model: Swami Vivekananda

Proudest moment: Having my children

Oft-repeated quote: 'Let's see how bad the bad luck is.'

Most Inspiring book/author: Bhagvad Gita, Swami Vivekananda's writings

One big dream for tomorrow: Way too many to achieve; my own TV show

Three must-haves for aspiring female entrepreneurs:

- Transparency: The playing field is not set for women but they can set it up for themselves.
- Persistence: There is no substitute to hard work.
- Forget balance, enjoy creating massive shifts.

NEERU SHARMA

Entrepreneur
Co-founder, Infibeam.com

Co-founder and director:	Infibeam.com
Education:	Alumna of Carnegie Mellon University—Tepper School of Business
Past corporate avatar:	Amazon, Alcatel Development India, Tata Consultancy Services
Just when you thought you had heard it all:	Regularly featured among the top ten women leading technology start-ups

A ROAD LESS TRAVELLED

Neeru swore off entrepreneurship early and not without good reason. Growing up, she had witnessed the fallout of her father's struggles as an entrepreneur and its impact on a middle-class household. Leading the life of a corporate warrior and earning a steady pay became her only ambition.

Yet, entrepreneurship beckoned later on in life as she went on to co-found a multimillion-dollar venture, Infibeam. It has been a long journey—one that has changed her manifold as a professional but kept her grounded as a person. Here's a walk-through.

'There is no passion to be found playing small'—Nelson Mandela

Walking into the office of Infibeam, if I was expecting a swanky set-up typical of funded start-ups, I couldn't have been further away from the truth. Set in upscale Gurgaon, this is a spartan office, a befitting set-up for an outlier in the e-tailing space, whose strategy seems to challenge regular norms.

I am directed to the office of the co-founder and head of corporate and business development, Neeru Sharma. An unabashed admirer of her mother, this is a real-life example of the torch of entrepreneurship being passed from one generation of woman entrepreneur to another though not in the traditional sense of handing over a business empire. While her mother was forced to take the entrepreneurial route, on account of the family falling upon bad times financially, Neeru's journey as an entrepreneur is one of unbridled passion.

'I come from a very middle-class family,' is her opening statement as we settle in to probe how early the seeds of entrepreneurship were sown in her life. Financial pressures at home forced out all other dreams, and growing up, Neeru's only aim in life was to earn enough to support her family. There was nothing to suggest back then that she would one day be at the helm of a thriving business valued at thousands of crores. Yet, now she is an unequivocal champion of entrepreneurship, even mentoring budding women entrepreneurs. No mean feat for someone who learnt early in life that entrepreneurship is fraught with risk and that the impact of a failed enterprise can be crushing for a middle-class family with limited financial muscle.

Back then in the late eighties, her father, bitten by the entrepreneurial bug, gave up a well-paying corporate job to start his own manufacturing venture—an auto lamps–manufacturing unit—but he had clearly not factored in the risks associated with it. Neeru recounts how business losses started mounting and bankruptcy loomed. How the family even got to know of the financial crisis plaguing their lives, is a tale worth telling in itself, both for its pathos and for its indication of the deep-seated societal norms that insist on portraying the male member as not just the primary breadwinner but also the protector insulating his family from financial trouble. An inkling that all was not well in their world rang by way of an innocuous phone call; her father answered it disguising his voice to keep creditors at bay. Overhearing the conversation, her mother had to cajole her husband into sharing the extent of his problems with the family.

I realize that grit and determination are in her DNA as Neeru narrates how her mother, fiercely protective of her family, took over a struggling business while her father returned to his corporate job to keep the home fires burning. She was not daunted by the fact that she had never been a professional and had absolutely no idea about running a manufacturing unit. The livelihood of forty workers depended on her leadership and she took up the challenge like a seasoned professional. To this day, there is a twinge of pride in her father as he recounts how his wife turned out to be a much better entrepreneur than him.

Times remained tough for a while, with her mother taking care of the business and her father working as a salaried employee. With two other siblings, money certainly remained in short supply through her early years but what she got aplenty was oodles of confidence and self-assurance to face any challenge head-on.

When asked who her biggest inspiration is, she replies instinctively, 'My mom.' An entrepreneur born out of sheer need, she gave Neeru the confidence that one can achieve anything with single-minded dedication and hard work. The axiom for her was that entrepreneurship arising out of passion and not just need had twice as many chances of success.

As a youngster, there was only one thought: how to contribute to home finances; which is why when the time came for Neeru to choose her field of study, the fact that computer engineers received a decent pay cheque was a clincher. Computer engineering led to the beginning of a corporate career driven by big brands and bigger pay cheques.

It is uncanny how the direction of Neeru's career and her marriage are inextricably linked to each other. While at college, Neeru found her biggest support in Anuj, her not-so-soon-to-be husband. For sure, they hung out together but thought of each other more as best buddies rather than as special someones. It was only during her post-graduation, when she left for her training at the Kolkata office of TCS and he stayed back in Delhi to prepare for his GRE, that separation pangs hit them hard. Matters reached a climax when she returned to Delhi post her training and was confronted by her father with an array of marriage proposals. Her reasoning was simple: 'You cannot expect me to marry someone I hardly know.' Her father's retort was simpler: 'In that case, marry someone you know.' The reference to Anuj was unmistakable. A quick parent-to-parent meeting settled matters. Anuj left soon after to pursue his master's from the University of Southern California. This was way back in 2001, their relationship surviving the long distance and culminating in marriage in 2005. The camaraderie is palpable as she talks of their relationship.

Coming back to Neeru's career trajectory, both she and her husband came from hard-core technology backgrounds and had not given much thought to their future beyond pursuing careers in this domain. It was her husband's father, himself an entrepreneur with investments in real estate, who first suggested that they consider setting up their own business. She says that the suggestion brought into sharp focus her early brush with the risks associated with entrepreneurship. If there was one lesson she had learnt for life, it was that one needs to be fully equipped before taking the plunge. At this stage, she felt she did not have a holistic view as her experience was limited to the technology domain alone. Her strong resolve of not jumping into the entrepreneurial bandwagon unprepared can be gauged from the fact that both she and her husband decided to first pursue a course in business management from an American college of repute to equip themselves with the necessary business overview.

So it came about that within three months of their marriage, while most couples would still be honeymooning, Neeru and her husband spent all their waking hours buried deep in books preparing for their GMAT exams. Their single-minded focus paid off with admission letters from two prestigious colleges in the US. The next two years of life as students of Carnegie Mellon were in Neeru's words some of the 'best years of my life'. She recalls the semi-bohemian lifestyle typical of student life with 'a bare minimum apartment, little money, no car but lots of friends and banter'.

Neeru followed studying management with working at Amazon, while her husband turned into an angel investor. Neeru absolutely loved the entrepreneurial culture that so defined working at Amazon, and wistfully reminisces the incredible ways in which the organization encouraged employees to explore new ideas. The stint with Amazon was memorable for more than one reason, this was also the place where she met her current team of co-founders—Vishal Mehta, Vijaya Kumar Subramanian and Sachin Oswal.

Vishal Mehta, a Cornell and MIT Sloan alumnus, was the first among them to move back to India, driven by the dream of founding a technology company.

When asked what makes corporate workers tick in the US, the land of opportunity, she points out that work passion is a big clincher. Appearing for a job interview at Amazon, for instance, she was pleasantly surprised by the fact that the interview comprised of a single question: 'What do you know about Amazon?' No technical test, no elaborate case studies to solve, nothing. With her degree from Carnegie Mellon, her competency was a given and they were more interested in establishing how driven she was as an individual. She had a similar experience while appearing for a job in front of the CEO of a top US organization. Extremely nervous about being face-to-face with the CEO of a blue-chip company, she was surprised 'when he handed over a blank sheet and pen and exited the room'. With no subject mentioned, her mind drew a blank for several minutes till the old fighting spirit returned and her essay on how she wanted to be a part of the insurance sector as they 'give something to smile even when devastating events happen around you', cracked the job for her. Other things being equal, passion, she feels, is the one overriding criteria for professional success, be it as an employee or an entrepreneur.

Amazon turned out to be the perfect training ground for her. As a part of the mergers and acquisitions team, she scoped out India and knew that the e-commerce industry in the country was set to explode within the next ten years. Her husband had already turned part-time entrepreneur by then, working actively with start-ups in the retail space, hand-holding and mentoring them to grow and expand their business. That India would be the home for their children had been a given, which is why when Neeru gave birth to her elder daughter, it seemed time to return to the family fold.

When asked if there was any fear in leaving a thriving corporate career to come back to India to chart a new course, that too, one where she had a lot of apprehensions earlier, she gives you a glimpse of her never-say-die attitude. 'Though business success cannot be predicted, I had done the next best thing—prepared myself meticulously,' she says, 'both through my course that gave me a strong foundation as well as through a detailed study of the Indian market.' As if to seal the decision the husband–wife duo fixed a date and booked their return flight to India, working backwards from there to wind up things in the US. Their experience with other Indian couples had taught them that unless a firm return date is set, procrastination sets in, something that they didn't want to fall prey to.

With return to India in motion, Neeru decided to start scouting for opportunities, which is when she reconnected with Vishal Mehta who was already in Ahmedabad and working on a business plan. The core team of founders got together; the fact that they had all worked together before, turned out to be a blessing. 'Since each of us had witnessed first-hand the capabilities of the other, our confidence in each other was high and that is one of the reasons why we are able to operate so effectively.'

The initial years were far from easy though. She tells how Infibeam's first Delhi office at Daryaganj was smaller than her current cubicle. She recalls the first sales call that she made to a publisher, a far cry from her corporate avatar. Even before she could sell the idea, she remembers spelling out the name INFIBEAM, a name nobody knew back then. It took some time for the concept to catch on, as it was a completely alien business model to hitherto brick-and-mortar sellers. Her experience at Amazon and degree from Carnegie Mellon though acted as a passport to open quite a few doors. When asked if being a woman entrepreneur she faced any prejudices along the way, she admits that while there were many challenges as a start-up, 'being a woman has not made it easy or tough to undertake entrepreneurship'.

The initial targets were modest—to be able to attract a couple of big clients to adopt the site, paving the way for others to follow. The distributor network grew from there and soon enough they were scaling up the team size to handle the increased workload, hiring category managers, vendor managers and the technical support team, following it up with another floor in the same building as they started running out of space. Infibeam has since seen exponential growth exploiting its first-mover advantage to capture a sizeable share of the market.

When quizzed about the current situation with very aggressive competition, their frequent rounds of funding (while Infibeam has chosen to remain by and large self-funded) and bigger market cap, what you get from her is an extremely composed reply. The team of co-founders has this 'one overriding vision', she says, 'to build an inclusive e-commerce ecosystem rather than just being an online destination through price wars.' Gearing up towards being the first e-commerce company to launch an IPO, Infibeam has clearly cut new grounds.

This kind of professional growth comes at a cost, of course. Her own success formula is to get her priorities right and decide which 'aspects of life can be delegated while I focus on the uncompromisable'. 'The concept of doing it all is a myth,' she says, pointing out that life itself is a series of optimizations. 'To take up more than one can chew, to not delegate, is a sure-shot formula for burnout.'

As far her personal life goes, she confesses that living in a joint family does make things a little easier for her. She says, 'Grandparents have this subtle way of passing on enduring values while as parents, we find ourselves cast more in the role of disciplinarians.' But that does not mean that she does not have her brush with working woman's guilt or that work–life balance is not a juggle for her. Time management is something she has learnt to hone. Years of experience as an entrepreneur have taught her that 'when you have less time to spend, you end up using it well'.

When asked about her greatest moments of pride in this long journey from completely closing the door to entrepreneurship to being hailed as a successful entrepreneur, her eyes shine as she recalls the time when her elder daughter told her that she wants to grow up to be just like her mom. For Neeru, it was like a flashback to the days when she wanted to emulate her own mother. The pride is unmistakable as she tells me how her daughters are fully clued into her work and talk about e-commerce without batting an eyelid. Their repertoire of terminology has also expanded to include 'co-working and venture capital' with their dad's foray into these fields. Her only advice to her daughters when she hears their different ambitions every day is to give their best in whatever they choose to be, even if it is to be a homemaker. With inspiration up close, this is a task the girls are certainly likely to live up to. As for Neeru's mother, it is her time now to bask in the glory of her daughter's success. Neeru smiles as she recalls how her mother, her earliest inspiration and her father-in-law who first sowed the seeds of entrepreneurship in the daughter-in-law, called up all their relatives, the first time she was scheduled to appear on a television show as a successful entrepreneur.

When asked about her future plans, she sees herself taking up a more active role mentoring women aspiring towards entrepreneurship. Her advice to budding women entrepreneurs is simple: 'Nothing works unless you do. If you have an idea and you keep persevering it with passion, there is nothing that can stand between you and success.' Point out the many perils of living in an EMI economy and she admits that there are brass tacks to consider while taking the plunge and that married into a family of entrepreneurs, her risk-taking ability was higher. 'Irrespective of individual circumstances, there is no substitute for meticulous planning,' she cautions. There is no mistaking the conviction in her tone as she goes on to add that 'despite your best efforts, if at worst the idea you started out with does not succeed, you would have learnt so much in your journey that you would have achieved something alternative or even bigger than you set out to.'

A firm believer in the maxim 'add life to moments instead of moments to life', she has certainly turned this belief into a fine art as she wants to enrich the lives of many more women. 'We need more women up there,' she says with determination. There is no mistaking her genuineness as she tells you that when she interacts with budding entrepreneurs who are passionate about their projects and are willing to give it their all, she knows that the only difference between them and her is that they have a 'different time curve, a different trajectory of success'. Soon they will be where she is and will be lending their hand to other women entrepreneurs.

As we wind up our meeting, her parting advice to women entrepreneurs is: 'Forget the fact that you are a woman. You are person with a great idea. Let us work towards an even platform where ideas are weighed, and passion and diligence are rewarded.'

Neeru has a job cut out for me as well. The next book, she says, has to be about the challenges of entrepreneurship itself without the gender aspect of it. Let me just say amen to that and to a world of equal opportunities.

WORDS OF WISDOM

- 'Being a woman has not made it easy or tough to undertake entrepreneurship.'
- 'You need to decide which aspects of life can be delegated while you focus on the uncompromisable.'
- 'The concept of doing it all is a myth.'
- 'To take up more than one can chew, to not delegate, is a sure-shot formula for burnout.'
- 'When you have less time to spend, you end up doing it well.'
- 'Nothing works unless you do.'
- 'If you have an idea and you keep persevering it with passion, there is nothing that can stand between you and success.'
- 'Despite your best efforts, if at worst, the idea you started out with does not succeed, you would have learnt so much in your journey that you would have achieved something alternative or even bigger than what you set out to do.'
- 'Add life to moments instead of moments to life.'
- 'We need more women up there.'
- 'Forget the fact that you are a woman. You are a person with a great idea.'

Snapshot

Birth sign: Scorpio

Biggest role model: My mother

Proudest moment: First interview on TV

Oft-repeated quote: 'Nothing will work unless you do.'

Favourite downtime activity: Spending time with my kids

Most inspiring book/author: *Blue Ocean Strategy*

One big dream for tomorrow: To build and run an institution for a social cause

Three must-haves for aspiring female entrepreneurs: Passion, networking, perseverance

SWATI KAUSHAL

Bestselling author

Published works:	*Piece of Cake*, *A Girl Like Me*, *Drop Dead* and *Lethal Spice*
Education:	Alumna of Indian Institute of Management, Calcutta
Past corporate avatar:	Brand manager with Nestlé India and Nokia
Honours and awards:	Femina L'Oreal 2013 Women of Worth Award
Just when you thought you had heard it all:	Hailed as the Indian Agatha Christie

NO GIRL LIKE HER

When you are an IIM Calcutta graduate, a high-flying corporate career is a given. So it was for Swati Kaushal who stepped out of its hallowed portals with a plan to revolutionize the world of marketing 'one limited offer at a time'. Several years of brand management for global companies later, came the inevitable juggling act of her corporate career and her role as a new mother. The everyday struggle to achieve that elusive balance led her to the realization that she didn't want to spend the day running the corporate rat race only to contend with guilt at the end of it. The decision to take a break from corporate life turned out to be a blessing in disguise; it led Swati to rediscover her passion for writing.

Fate continued to tempt her though. While writing her first book, Swati received a job offer most would jump at. To the immense dismay of sceptics—and there were many—her passion for writing prevailed over corporate lure. A decision she has not rued since. Today she derives her greatest joy writing bestsellers, which celebrate women role models. Surely the switchover wasn't a 'piece of cake'. This is a story of her strife and rediscovery of her own self.

'Intuition is seeing with the soul'—Dean Koontz, author

Waiting for my Skype call to connect with Swati Kaushal in faraway Connecticut, I am curious to know what led this IIM grad to turn into a full-time author. If I was hoping to hear a story where amidst a high-flying marketing career, she felt creative pangs that led her to quit her day job, it would only be half the story. In Swati's tale is also hidden the tale of several women who contend with mid-career breaks. Only few like Swati have the resilience to turn their passions into their careers, the *second* time around!

I get a taste of her gutsy spirit early in the conversation when an innocuous discussion about children's books leads her to reveal that as a child, she preferred Gretel over Cinderella because Gretel had the temerity to kick the witch's butt while Cinderella waited for the prince to rescue her. Much of her childhood was spent happily fantasizing about being an astronaut, who explored outer space to make exciting discoveries. 'I guess I always did love to merge fantasy with reality, even at an early age,' she says good-humouredly. As a child, she recalls waiting for the nightly storytelling sessions when she would hear her grandfather's rich voice weave out tales of princesses and warriors. She vividly remembers this one incident when her grandfather had just begun an enchanting story of twelve princesses and three rakshasas, when he had to attend to some unexpected guests. As the eldest of her cousins, the task of completing the story was entrusted to Swati. Giving free rein to her imagination, in that one tale, she weaved twelve unique tales, one for each princess. The expression of delight on her cousins' faces was reward enough for Swati, who by her own admission, was 'the quiet girl with the explosion of subversive ideas bubbling behind a pair of nerdy glasses'.

When it came to choosing a career for herself, admission to the prestigious Indian Institute of Management, Calcutta, opened the doors to a whole new world of opportunities. IIM turned out to be a milestone in more ways than one; it not only laid the groundwork for an illustrious corporate career but also gave her a life partner in the form of a batchmate. She recounts how, at the entrance interview for IIM Ahmedabad, Vivek happened to be the first person to come out of the interview room. As other aspirants crowded around him, curious to know about his experience, she remembers him laughing his head off, taking just about enough breaks in between to tell everyone that it was the worst interview of his life. Swati recalls how his laughter kind of defused the tense atmosphere in the room and endeared the young man to her. The two of them met again, this time as new joinees at IIM Calcutta. Cupid struck sometime in those two years, otherwise filled with projects and grade-point averages. They have been married for twenty years now.

The years immediately after IIM were hectic to say the least, dedicated to excelling in the corporate rat race. Joining as a trainee, Swati quickly rose through the ranks to become a brand manager at a large MNC. She recalls how in those years, female presence in high-pressure brand and marketing jobs was still limited, and there was a time when in one of her assignments, she was the only female in an office full of men. Uncomfortable as she was with all the smoking, swearing and cursing that was part of this all-male office, the message to her was loud and clear: 'You need to adjust to our ways.'

It was the birth of her first child that changed Swati's world. Juggling roles as a corporate warrior and a mother became an everyday necessity as the demands of professional life continued unabated. Discuss work–life balance with her and she rues the fact that society comes down hard on working mothers. The working mother's guilt became something that she had to contend with every day. As if her own guilt trip wasn't enough, she recalls instances when despite the support of her husband, people were quick to pronounce judgement when a demanding work schedule meant leaving the baby behind for long hours. 'Despite societal progress,' she says, 'there are many subliminal messages being sent that demand women to be the primary caregivers and men to be the chief bread earners,' near non-existent paternity leave, being one of them. She points out how in certain Scandinavian countries, three years of leave is earmarked for new parents, which they can take in turns, irrespective of gender, without adversely impacting either of their careers. For Swati, however, an incident where her child was down with pneumonia and had to be hospitalized led her to take the bold decision to take some time off from her corporate career; living this compartmentalized life steeped in guilt was not for her.

While mid-career breaks are a hard reality for women facing lack of flexibility and access to childcare, I am curious to know how the decision of taking a career break worked out for someone who had a dream run of academic and professional success. With more than a hint of laughter in her voice, she says that the initial years of quitting were tougher on her parents; they found it hard to digest the reality of their daughter giving up a thriving career built with so much labour.

When asked about her own fears of giving up her identity as a successful corporate executive, she says, 'The initial fears that come with any change were certainly potent as corporate life had become an intrinsic part of my identity. But what I also came to realize was that it wasn't just taking care of my child that led me to this decision, although it was a sizeable part. Somewhere deep within me was this growing recognition that life was too short to not follow one's heart. This desire kept me going in the days following my quitting as I set to rediscover myself.'

Free of corporate baggage, spending time with her little bundle became a daily source of joy, but there remained this 'burning desire' to do something worthwhile with her talent. Writing had always been her first love, travelling with her in some form or shape all through her life journey. Over the years, her writing had acquired a voice that was very contemporary and had even proved to be an invaluable asset to her professional career. She recalls that in her marketing role she had loved creating crisp brand tag lines that resonated well with the audience. Gut instinct told her that with her short and snappy prose, she could speak the voice of modern India.

At this critical juncture of self-discovery, a new job for her husband took the family to the US. Starting a whole new life in a faraway country, Swati recalls a morning when she sat reminiscing about some funny incidents from her corporate stint and decided to pen them down on a whim. They succeeded not only in eliciting laughs but also a strong recommendation from a journalist friend that she should turn it into a book. She took to the task, albeit with some trepidation. It soon gave way to confidence as once she settled down to writing, she says, 'It went quite fast, as books go.'

While she was busy spinning several twists in the tale, life was spinning its own twists for her. At this time came along a job offer with an online education company in the US that would pretty much qualify for the label of a 'dream job'—in line with her previous experience, replete with a fancy designation and a sizable pay cheque. Her child was a lot more settled now, so taking up the offer was a definite possibility; only her heart was no longer in it. She found herself pulled between the lure of a stable corporate job, something that she had spent years training for, and her love for writing, which others perceived as nothing more than a passing 'hobby'. In fact, she recalls how a number of well-wishers even pronounced her 'insane' for not jumping at the offer. Swati confesses that not taking up the offer when there was no certainty that her book would ever see the light of day did seem like a 'crazy' decision at the time. When asked how she ended up choosing a totally unknown road over a 'stable job', she says, 'It was as if I was guided by my intuition. I was in a zone where I felt it was my calling, where neither money nor security tended to matter.'

In making the decision to write though, 'I was opening myself to rejection and ridicule,' she admits. A role that many naysayers played to perfection! There were enough and more people reminding her that she was simply wasting her talent when she could be gainfully employed. 'It was a leap of faith that I took. I knew that if I did not write the book now, it would never get written,' she says, her voice jumping a notch. 'Besides, only I could write this book; this job on the other hand could be done by someone else.'

It is fitting to mention that the success of her debut work, *Piece of Cake*, silenced her critics. A witty amalgamation of nuances from both the corporate world and the Indian marriage market (both of which Swati had experienced first-hand), the book has been hailed as the Indian version of *Bridget Jones's Diary*. Since being first published, *Piece of Cake* has gone through six reprints and has been published in three languages.

When asked about her first experience as a published author, she reveals that it was 'strange but quite magical' to hold that first copy in her hand. 'Another particularly enduring memory that I have is when my second book, *A Girl Like Me*, released.' After reading this coming-of-age story dealing with teenage angst, a young girl wrote to Swati to tell her how the story helped her reconcile with her mom with whom she had always shared a love–hate relationship. 'It is the human element that makes it so real,' Swati says with unmistakable enthusiasm in her voice.

When quizzed on her views regarding the nomenclature of 'chick lit' fiction that her novels have been dubbed as a part of, she laughs and says, 'There could have been worse labels. But then do labels really matter as long as people relate to my work?' Making no bones about the fact that her books do not aspire to be a part of highbrow literary fiction, Swati adds, 'Both literary fiction and *aam aadmi* fiction have found their own niches.'

Moving on, with her subsequent books Swati made a successful foray into the genre of crime fiction. In developing the character of a tough female cop in Niki Marwah, Swati has not only urbanized the female Indian cop, but also explored the world view from the perspective of a woman in authority. When asked if creating strong women characters is a form of covert revolt against the stereotypes set for women in society, she admits that commercial success aside, she wants to create a body of work that celebrates women role models. The character of Niki Marwah exemplifies a strong message: 'It is not important for a woman to behave like a man to prove herself.' In her childhood, Swati recalls that anything girly was equated with being frivolous. As for Niki, if her love for shoes are anything to go by, she isn't afraid to be a woman in a man's world.

So, having come so far, does she look back on her corporate co-travellers, who have been steadily climbing the corporate ladder, with a feeling of nostalgia? 'The only thing that I miss is the hustle and bustle of corporate life; those ideations as a team. Writing is a lonely process, but of course, once the book is ready, and you can share it with the world, it is a completely surreal feeling. It makes up for all the isolation and agony, sweat and tears that went before,' she says.

Speaking of her writing process, she confesses to following a 'Me Hour' every morning. Waking up religiously at six, she walks in to her local Starbucks, their first visitor, and spends an hour planning her writing day, over a steaming cuppa. Therein lies her piece of advice for all women contemplating a career change: 'Create a space for yourself, come up with an actionable plan and then pursue it relentlessly without second-guessing yourself. Confronting your own fears is the first step to make things happen.' That was how she reconstructed her identity after giving up her corporate career.

To aspiring women writers, her advice is: 'Write fearlessly and simply be yourself.' She is quick to remind would-be authors that the 'real reward of writing is the "process" of creation . . . fame is just a by-product.'

As for herself, the 'process of creation' continues unabated; in her new venture, *My High School Mentor*, a go-to destination for college-bound students and their parents, she combines her three diverse worlds of marketing, writing and parenting. 'My world keeps getting busier and more and more meaningful,' she says.

There couldn't be a better closure to our conversation as she quotes Elizabeth Gilbert, the acclaimed author of *Eat Pray Love*, who had once said, 'Any talent that you don't use will become a burden over time, heavy and sad. Set it (and you) free.'

Swati has done just that!

WORDS OF WISDOM

- 'There are many subliminal messages being sent that demand women to be primary caregivers and men to be chief bread earners.'
- 'It was as if I was guided by my intuition. I was in a zone where I felt it was my calling, where neither money nor security tended to matter.'
- 'It was a leap of faith that I took. I knew that if I do not write the book now, it would never get written.'
- 'It is not important for a woman to behave like a man to prove herself.'
- 'It [a published book] is a completely surreal feeling. It makes up for all the isolation and agony, sweat and tears that went before.'
- 'There is a lot of sweat and enough sacrifices that go behind every success.'
- 'Write fearlessly and simply be yourself.'
- 'Create a space for yourself, come up with an actionable plan and then pursue it relentlessly without second-guessing yourself.'
- 'Confronting your own fears is the first step to make things happen.'
- 'When you're a woman, and you have energy, enthusiasm, passion and confidence, there is nothing you can't do!'
- 'Any talent that you don't use will become a burden over time, heavy and sad. Set it (and you) free'—Elizabeth Gilbert

Snapshot

Birth sign: Gemini

Biggest role model: During my growing-up years, my mother. Now, I just want to be ME.

Proudest moment: When people tell me I have raised an amazing child, and when fans tell me that my book has made a difference to their lives.

Oft-repeated quote: 'There's always the next play.'

Favourite downtime activity: Relaxing with a glass of wine.

Most inspiring book/author: Harry Potter series. The creativity simply blows me away.

One big dream for tomorrow: To leave a mark on the world

Three must-haves for aspiring female entrepreneurs: Extreme passion, unfailing confidence, ferocious energy.

DR RANGANA RUPAVI CHOUDHURI

International speaker, master trainer of coaching modalities and alternate therapies (EFT, NLP, Journey and Matrix Re-Imprinting)

Founder:	Vitality Living College
Education:	Alumna of Oxford University
Past corporate avatar:	Headed the marketing function at Smith and Nephew, an MNC engaged in medical equipment manufacturing, for over a decade

Just when you thought you had heard it all: Doctorate in cancer research

AN INTENSIVE JOURNEY

Armed with a PhD in cancer research from the prestigious Oxford University, Rangana entered the corporate bandwagon with a job at a global healthcare company, rising quickly through the ranks to become the only woman and the youngest member on its board. A decade into the corporate rat race, her wake-up call was when she was diagnosed with abnormal cell growth and a chronic hormonal condition. Defying her doctor's prognosis, she chose alternative healing to nurse herself back to health. This miraculous personal journey, in turn, sparked an interest that led her to study everything about alternative healing and coaching systems from masters around the world. The defining moment was when she left behind a highly successful corporate career to become a full-time practitioner. Today she finds her calendar full as she travels across the globe conducting well-received seminars that have created lasting changes in the lives of many. This is her journey.

'Boldness has genius, power and magic in it.
Begin it now'—Goethe, writer and statesman

A PhD in cancer research from Oxford University, a patent in baby formula and a published paper on cancer of the cervix to her credit! I was going through Rangana's impressive list of achievements yet another time while waiting to meet her at Zorba the Buddha, the lush venue for her coaching workshop in New Delhi, when she walked up to me exuding her trademark energy, dressed in vibrant blue.

'I love bright colours,' she quips as I compliment her. 'I used to wear a dark suit to work every day. Now my wardrobe is much more me, the colours reek of comfort yet formality, elegance yet opulence.' With that one sentence, she effortlessly steers us towards her career journey, a ride that is inspirational, to say the least.

Born in Singapore and having lived in Hong Kong, India, Luxembourg, the UK, Botswana, Zimbabwe and the USA, Rangana's initiation to different cultures and sensibilities began early. A large part of her childhood was spent at a boarding school in Great Britain while her parents were posted in Africa. She recalls that her first brush with the Indian education system was when she returned briefly to join an Indian school for her plus two. Much as she loves India and its rich tapestry, she confesses to struggling with rote memorizing the curriculum during those two years. A curious bent of mind (always the one with the most questions) found her heading to a university in England for a course in applied biology soon after.

Determined to fund her own education, she took a year off while in the UK, working for commercial set-ups such as Unilever as well as for the Cancer Research Campaign, bringing her a taste of both academia and corporate affairs, an experience that was to come in handy in later life. This was followed by a full scholarship to do a PhD in Cancer Research at Oxford University.

The years that followed saw Rangana live a frugal existence at Oxford University. 'I had a bike,' she says with a faraway look in her eyes, 'and stayed in a small room which was a far cry from a proper accommodation so that I could save some money to send back home to my parents. Despite all this I never felt a sense of need or want. Those were, in fact, enriching times.' With a PhD, she decided to enter the world of business, academia not really appealing to the doer in her.

'Marketing happened to me quite by chance,' she admits. 'I just happened to know of a vacancy in the planning department with a global medical equipment–manufacturing company.' Her full-throated laughter fills the room as she describes her first interview, when all starry-eyed she walked into the room, eager to get a taste of the business world. The very first question by the HR team on how she would add value to the role saw her going the full mile. An exhaustive explanation of how she would 'first plan the big picture and then get into details', had only reached about midway when she was cut short by the interviewer. She was told that the role involved crunching statistics and did not cover the expanse she was looking for. The interviewer was, however, impressed enough by her enthusiasm to not only suggest that she apply for a marketing role but also to arrange an interview for her.

That innocuous interview was the beginning of her long tryst with marketing, an area she knew nothing about, but soon grew to love. 'It was as if I had found my calling after years of research. Marketing gave me a whole new world— the customer piece, science, credibility, networking with medical doctors, everything seemed to come together into one challenging role,' she says.

After a two-year stint in the UK, her growing role in the organization led her to the sunny beaches of Florida. 'I witnessed a sharp climb at work. Not only was I financially successful, I was also the first and only female to be included in the company's board,' she says with an expression that is a curious mix of pride and humility.

The conversation takes a sombre turn as she recounts how she had always tended towards workaholism, driving herself hard. Amidst her busy routine, therefore, she was dismissive of the first signs of ill health, which she put down to fatigue and continued with her normal work schedule, until she was forced to visit the doctor, as the symptoms showed no signs of relenting. Her worst fear came true when she was diagnosed with abnormal cells and a chronic hormonal condition—the prognosis was not too good. The doctor recommended surgery, even asking her to get admitted immediately. There's no way I can miss the welling of her eyes as she tells me that this wasn't the end of her ordeal. The doctor also pronounced a sentence that 'felt so final'. Her reproductive system, she was told, was shutting down and she would not be able to bear children. Her voice drops to an inaudible whisper as she says, 'My identity as a woman was challenged in that one minute.' She confesses that, having learnt the news and driving by the sea, the expanse of the sea only mirrored the many questions that were running through her mind. Stripped of the opportunity of giving birth to a new life, Rangana questioned her very identity. She admits that one of the first thoughts to cross her mind was: 'Who would want to marry me?' In that one instance, she recalls, how she had mentally shut the door to marriage. Never one to wallow in self-pity, she, however, takes only an instant to pull herself together, and goes on to regale me with stories about the innovative excuses that she came up with, to reject the many prospective suitors her father kept bringing to her. The doctor's visit had proved to be decisive in more ways than one.

The irony isn't lost on me as she tells me that not so long ago, she was researching ways to prevent multiplication of cancer cells and now the very same cells had started invading her body, as if mocking her. Despite studying conventional medicine in depth and also making a career out of marketing it to others, she could not bring herself to go in for surgery. I was, however, not prepared to handle the shock of her next statement and my mouth refused to close as she told me that she kept the diagnosis a secret from everyone, and even continued her usual work pattern, as if in denial of the truth. All of this until her father's passing away brought her back to India and to a decisive point in her life.

The death of her father, she reminisces, brought about a 'huge spiritual awakening'. Cremating him made her realize that she was more than just a body inhabiting this earth. The realization led to something hitherto unheard-of in Rangana's work vocabulary—taking three weeks off from work to introspect. It was at this time that destiny intervened as she chanced upon a book called *The Journey*, by Brandon Bays, which recounted Bays's story of healing and reconciliation. 'I read it from cover to cover, crying through most of it,' she says. Mesmerized by Brandon's story of healing herself from a basketball-sized tumour by way of alternative therapy, Rangana felt positive for the first time since being diagnosed. Brandon had put into practice everything she had learnt about alternative healing, including 'nutrition, herbology, kinesiology, meditation and guided introspection with a carefully planned natural healing regimen' and healed herself without drugs and surgery.

It proved to be a huge turning point for Rangana as the book led her to 'explore the link between body and emotions between healing and health'. Her voice is heavily laced with irony as she tells me how life can change direction in seconds. 'Here I was, a PhD in cancer research who instinctively knew that there was something powerful in alternative therapy.'

After returning to work, she enrolled in The Journey course developed by Brandon Bays, which was a unique approach to awakening and cellular healing, the result of Brandon's continuous work on herself. Inspired by it, Rangana went on to do intensive inner work that 'led me to free the old emotional patterns and memories stored in our cells, and replace it with a healing energy'. What she managed to achieve in the process was to get rid of the abnormal cells destroying her body. It is nothing short of miraculous as she describes the subsequent visit to her doctor—the doctor's utter disbelief matching her sheer joy as the test results were negative for cancer. She had managed to heal her body completely, all this without conventional drugs or surgery! Not just that, her reproductive system had also opened up and was functioning normally.

Resuming her corporate role, Rangana spent the next seven years using every break that she took from work to study coaching and alternative healing from masters all over the world, including Brandon Bays, Byron Katie, John Seymour, Richard Bandler and Tony Robbins. 'Tony's course,' she says, 'was significant in helping me discover who I really was, it made me realize that I had moulded myself to suit my corporate role.' By the end of her quest, she had gained expertise in alternative healing and coaching techniques that included Emotional Freedom Technique, a form of psychological acupressure often known as 'tapping'; Neuro Linguistic Programing, a school of thought that studies the dynamics between mind (neuro) and language (linguistic) and their interplay, among others. 'In hindsight, not being married and not having children gave me the luxury to pursue my journey,' she adds thoughtfully.

On the work front, she confesses it was a great run as she grew the business from $5 million to $25 million in two years and worked across the globe, in countries such as France and Sweden, till destiny intervened again. A bad road accident left her with a broken pelvis and nine months of complete bed rest. 'The accident gave me time to reflect on what I really wanted from life,' she says. Immobilized and in excruciating pain, she decided to distract herself from the pain by listening to Wayne Dyer's audio tapes, a recuperating gift from her sister.

His use of the nursery rhyme 'row, row, row your boat gently down the stream' as a metaphor on how to live your life, touched a deep chord within Rangana. The realization that she wanted to row her own boat hit her hard. 'It made me realize that I was no longer feeling fulfilled in my corporate career and wanted to make a tangible difference in other people's lives,' she says.

With the realization dawning that 'just to be me is important and that I don't want to live a lie', Rangana decided to bid adieu to a promising career. 'The first thing I did after I quit my job was to book tickets to Hawaii for my mom and myself,' she says animatedly. 'I realized how little time I had spent with her and it was time to make amends.'

When asked about the aftermath of quitting, she admits to a host of lifestyle changes. She recalls how she had to give up her car and downsize to a humble apartment. 'There was always the worry about not being able to pay bills,' she says. When asked if she also faced a host of naysayers in this journey, she laughs aloud. 'The only naysayer in my life is me,' she says, a wealth of wisdom hidden beneath her chirpiness.

Already a trained coach, Rangana had started coaching private clients by this time, though the money was nowhere enough to cover her bills. 'I spent a year doubting myself,' she admits. As news of her resignation spread, headhunters started courting her for leadership roles similar to her last stint. Not yet fully reconciled with her changed status, she attended several interviews, till one particular interview effectively put the brakes on her return to corporate life once and for all. There couldn't be a better visual imagery than her description of this interview. 'This final round was with a psychologist,' she recounts. 'To his question, "how do you take decisions?", my answer came instinctively—with my gut. In that one moment, I knew that I had lost the job. What I also knew was that I couldn't change myself to fit a particular role. Stepping out, as I closed the door of the room, I also closed the door to any thoughts of going back to the corporate world,' she adds. She recounts how on her flight back home when she ordered lemonade at the airport, it tasted like 'the first lemonade of freedom'.

I am soon regaled by her characteristic wit as she recounts her first Journey seminar, this time as a full-time practitioner. She recalls how before the start of the seminar she found asking herself, 'What the hell were you thinking when you agreed to do this?' I can't help laughing as she tells me how she was fervently praying that the side of her who organized the seminar better show up. Paralysed with fear she was wistfully recalling her old life and thinking, 'How life would have been better sitting behind a laptop.' And yet, when it was time for her to go on stage, 'everything was presented from Grace—it was as if I had no body, no mind and was just an empty vessel through which magic just happened. To this day I am in awe,' she adds.

One cannot help admiring this lady who has come a long way since then, not only successfully turning her own life around but personally touching the lives of over 4000 people with her live interventions, trainings and one-to-one sessions, creating lasting positive transformations. Today she travels around the world enabling personal, professional and spiritual development. She is now on a mission to create 1000 trainers worldwide to be able to make these skills available to impact the lives of many others.

When quizzed on what she considers her greatest learning during this journey of self-healing and thereafter healing many others, she gets into a reflective mood. She says that she believes that the knowledge that 'my past doesn't equal my future' relieved her of the burden of living up to past expectations.

As someone who has experienced the highs of success both in her corporate avatar as well as in her present role, I am curious to know if success and widespread recognition have changed her in any way. Infinitely wiser than her years, she tells me how having given up wanting 'significance', she isn't attached to the idea of success any more—the idea of empowering people and being of service being a bigger lure. Having achieved 'infinite inner peace that never comes and goes, but is always there', the term 'success' now sounds clichéd to her.

'What about looking back at your corporate fellow travellers? Is the feeling that of nostalgia or retribution?' I ask.

She laughs and says that when she looks at black suits on their way to work, she cannot help but feel lucky for the life she now leads—the reference to her own bright clothes, unmistakable. She even has an orange day earmarked on her calendar, amidst her hectic schedule, when she likes to unwind by watching movies, getting a spa treatment or meeting close friends and family. 'I am living the life I always wanted to. Learning to say no to work to spend time with my mom is a seismic shift from my workaholic corporate days,' she remarks.

What is her advice to women sitting on the entrepreneurial fence? 'Be clear about your own truth and act on it,' she says. 'You don't want to be eighty and think "if only I had done that". My own wake-up call was my health. You need to find your own purpose.'

'What about all the fears that precede a change? Aren't they potent too?' I probe. 'Purpose is more valuable than fear,' she retorts immediately. 'Is being fearful the way you want your children to remember you?' she asks rhetorically, laying all my questions to rest.

Just as our conversation is drawing to a close, she reminds me of one of her favourite quotes: 'Whatever you can do or dream you can, begin it. Boldness has genius, power and magic in it. Begin it now.' As for herself, she continues to spread her magic seminar after seminar.

WORDS OF WISDOM

- 'Just to be me was important. I didn't want to live a lie. I wanted to be true to myself.'
- 'The only naysayer in my life is me.'
- 'My past doesn't equal my future.'
- '[I have] infinite inner peace that never comes and goes, it is always there.'
- 'My own wake-up call was my health. You need to find your own purpose.'
- 'Be clear about your own truth and act on it.'
- 'Purpose is more valuable than fear. Is being fearful the way you want your children to remember you?'

Snapshot

Birth sign: Scorpio

Biggest role model: My mother

Proudest moment: When I got my PhD from Oxford

Oft-repeated quote: 'Until one is committed, there is hesitancy, the chance to draw back, always.'

Favourite downtime activity: Combining my spiritual interests with travel

Most inspiring book/author: *Monk Who Sold his Ferrari*, *The Alchemist*

One big dream for tomorrow: Live it now

Three must-haves for aspiring female entrepreneurs:

- Be clear about your truth and act on it.
- Set boundaries, don't say yes when you mean to say no.
- Whatever you do, don't forget to be grateful.

POOJA WARIER

Social entrepreneur
Co-founder, UnLtd India-Launchpad for Social Entrepreneurs

Co-founder and CEO:	UnLtd India, a launchpad for social entrepreneurs Bombay Connect, a collaborative space for people with passion for positive social change

	Journeys for Change, immersive journeys to help leaders make greater impact
Past corporate avatar:	MV Foundation, World Social Forum, Comet Media
Education:	Alumna of Tata Institute of Social Sciences
Honours and awards:	Awarded as a Young Global Leader by World Economic Forum, 2013; TED India Fellow, frequent speaker on national and international forums
Just when you thought you had heard it all:	Featured among the top ten upcoming female entrepreneurs in India

THE CHANGE MAKER

Abandoned by her father when she was twelve and raised by a fiercely independent single mother, Pooja Warier's relationship with money was formed early; she knew it was meant to ebb and flow. Moving from one career assignment to another, she finally found her calling in social entrepreneurship at the age of twenty-six. To the many who felt that she was taking too much of a career risk in jumping on to the near non-existent social entrepreneurship space in India, her rejoinder was matter of fact: 'Money is important to survive, attachment with it is not.'

Today, her venture, UnLtd India, has worked with more than 200 young social entrepreneurs, helping them grow and positively impact the lives of communities in which they operate. Driven by the will to turn India into a hotbed of social innovation, Pooja is a well-respected spokesperson for female entrepreneurship on the world stage. This is an account of her journey of change.

'Progress is impossible without change'—George Bernard Shaw, playwright

Nothing, not even reading her long list of accomplishments, could have prepared me for my meeting with Pooja Warier. Here is a woman who has chosen not to be cowed down by the challenges life chose to throw her way, rising instead to become a huge role model of professional success. She not only has three successful ventures (UnLtd India, Bombay Connect, Journeys for Change) to her credit, but is also a mentor and guide to hundreds of social entrepreneurs aiming to bring about a wider social change. If there is one line that can aptly summarize her achievements, it is that 'success comes from not giving up on yourself'.

Born to a Christian mother and a Hindu father, she was brought up in a fairly progressive atmosphere where her parents consciously chose not to follow any one religion, allowing Pooja the freedom to define her own relationship with God and pretty much everything else.

Life with a generous, loving father and a strong, independent and supportive mother went by happily for the first twelve years till a momentous event changed her life forever. To this day, she does not know why her father chose to walk out on them with neither any notice nor any explanation, leaving her mother, a housewife, to take over the reins of the household.

There is visible pride as she narrates how her mother 'set aside her personal grief to provide for herself and her daughter'. They ended up selling a lot of household stuff to make ends meet, even moving in to another house in a not-so-great locality, till her mother managed to secure a job that ensured a stable livelihood. The incident left an indelible mark on young Pooja's mind about, both the necessity and limitations of money. While money was essential for survival, she came to a conclusion early on, that it had no permanence, and attachment to it was pointless. An important part of her relationship with money was also the realization that there is money available in the ecosystem: 'All you need to know is how to acquire it and then how to make the best use of it.'

Hugely inspired by her mother's determination and courage in the face of obstacles, she learnt that human life is made up of endless possibilities. 'Living in north India, with a single mother, where most people lived in huge families, taught me that it is okay to be different,' she says in the most matter-of-fact manner.

Her fascination for exploring uncharted territories started early with a childhood dream of wanting to be an astronomer. What could have been a promising career exploring what lies beyond the planet we inhabit, ended abruptly 'when realization dawned that being a space explorer involved studying physics, and mathematics and a whole lot of numbers'. More inclined towards behavioural sciences than mathematics, Pooja chose to explore the human mind, and pursued a major in psychology.

When asked what led her to Tata Institute of Social Sciences (TISS) to study social work, she chuckles and tells me how it was a 'huge mistake'. She confesses how the nomenclature of the course at TISS—criminology and correctional work—led her to be hugely excited with the prospect of understanding the inner workings of a criminal mind. Add to it the fact that she was going to be away from small-town Chandigarh for the first time and join TISS in Mumbai, sealed the decision. However, after her very first class, to her dismay, she realized that the course was more about correctional work and had very little to do with criminology. Not wanting to give up, as she had taken up the course against the wishes of her mother, who, like most parents, wanted her daughter to pursue IAS or medicine, Pooja started using her free time to attend all possible lectures at college, even those that weren't part of her course. 'Fate has a way of intervening in unexpected ways,' she says. 'I ended up studying developmental work by accident rather than by choice.'

Mumbai, with its cosmopolitan outlook and constant churn of ideas, soon became home for her. Her first job after TISS was with an organization that worked with street children, mentally challenged kids and young adults in urban Mumbai. A few months into the job, Pooja realized that getting these children off the streets involved a lot more than just teaching them job-related skills. Another reality that hit her was that while the founder of the organization was extremely passionate about the project, for her it was just a paid job. Realizing that the children deserved someone who was passionate about the cause and that she herself needed to discover work that she would be passionate about, she decided to call it quits.

The next couple of years went by in trying to discover her true calling. She worked with the World Social Forum and then with an educational organization that was organizing festivals to showcase innovation in education and teaching methodologies. In hindsight, in moving from one job to another, 'it was as if I was searching for something . . . building a list of what I wanted to do and what I did not want to do.'

It was while organizing one of these education festivals that Pooja met Michael Norton, the founding trustee of UnLtd UK, which 'supports individuals who have their ventures firmly rooted in delivering positive social change'. This was a meeting that proved to be fortuitous. Keen to explore opportunities outside India, Pooja inquired about work opportunities at UnLtd UK. The reply was prompt—UnLtd UK was looking for someone from India who could help it arrange a learning tour of the country for their awardees and she might fit the bill. Pooja soon found herself in the offices of UnLtd UK, which she says had an atmosphere 'beyond what I had expected or even imagined'.

With a massive 1-million-pound endowment and four highly charged office floors, UnLtd UK operated on a huge scale. The office was packed with young people, all of whom were upbeat and enthusiastic about the work that they were doing. Pooja loved the free exchange of ideas and interesting discussions that a constant stream of young, budding entrepreneurs kept bringing to the office every minute of the day. She confesses how she found the whole concept of people walking into the office to seek money absolutely alien, as was the concept of recognizing young people as vehicles of change.

But she soon realized that this was exactly the work that she wanted to do. Most importantly, 'I loved who I became with them.' Looking for similar organizations in India to work with, she was surprised to find only a handful of them. It soon became clear that there was a space for something like UnLtd in India. She got enthusiastic support from Richard, her boss, when she first broached the topic with him; Richard went on to become a co-founder while Michael Norton came on board as the founding trustee. Next, they decided to shoot off a mail to the UnLtd UK's CEO requesting support to set up similar operations in India. While the idea seemed wonderful, UnLtd UK did not have a mandate to expand operations outside the UK. However, trust and respect won over, and the CEO allowed them to use the concept as well as the UnLtd brand name in India.

When asked if she was afraid of giving up the familiar for the unknown, she reminds me, 'Money is important to survive, attachment with it is not.' She says that while she did encounter many who felt it was too risky a proposition, she was sure that she had found her original calling.

That said, she never had thought of turning entrepreneur. The initial plan was to join a host organization willing to support her in launching UnLtd India under its umbrella. Not looking for monetary support but rather institutional support at this stage, Pooja and Richard were themselves willing to take up the job of fundraisers. They soon realized their naiveté as organization after organization rejected their proposal, citing it to be too risky, or imposed restrictions on how the programme would support proven entrepreneurs. This opened their eyes to the fact that few organizations had an understanding of how social entrepreneurship worked, and getting support for an idea based on social impact was going to be difficult at best.

Understanding that organizational support would be hard to come by, Pooja and Richard decided to turn entrepreneurs themselves and launched UnLtd India in 2007. Fundraising was the big obstacle to cross and after attending more than fifty meetings and fielding questions such as 'What do we do if the person ran away with our money?', they were frustrated with the process. When asked if the idea of giving up and going back to a salaried job crossed her mind, she says, 'The more rejections we got, the more determined we became, because it just clearly showed that there was a gap that UnLtd India could bridge successfully.' Rejections only reinforced their determination that the market had not woken up to the potential of social entrepreneurship and needed an organization like UnLtd India to set the ball rolling.

There were people who openly questioned whether such a model could work in India, their premise being that people in the UK had money and could afford the luxury of quitting jobs and starting a social venture. The scene in India, they said, was different. In fact, Pooja was challenged to find her first investees; she took up the challenge and found three such investees who were 'poster kids of the kind of social entrepreneurship I had been speaking about'.

Today, UnLtd India has supported over 200 social entrepreneurs, impacted 1.17 million beneficiaries and created 12,000 jobs. For each rupee that UnLtd has provided in funding, their investees have raised or earned 14.5 rupees—a whopping 1450 per cent increase.

When asked what she finds most gratifying in the journey personally, she reflects for a while before answering. The success of the venture apart, she was more pleased with the transformation in the personality of investees through their entrepreneurial journey. Many of them had walked into her office big on dreams but lacking in confidence; only to be transformed into confident, articulate and powerful leaders. Lending credibility, support and funds to a worthy venture 'can work wonders', she points out, as it did in the case of Ashok Rathod, for example, a young dynamic son of a migrant fisherman in Colaba. When Pooja first met him, Ashok was just nineteen and organized football sessions in his neighbourhood as a way to encourage children to stay in school and learn life skills. Today, at the age of twenty-five, as a FIFA community partner, he trains organizations across the world and is invited for talks globally. All this has been made possible with a little help from UnLtd India. Ashok's case goes a long way in supporting Pooja's theory that 'social entrepreneurs can and must be found in communities living in adversity as much as those living in abundance.'

The environment, she admits, is now more supportive of social entrepreneurship than when she first began seven years ago. For one, there are a lot more people who want to become social entrepreneurs, unlike the days when UnLtd India found it a struggle to identify even ten quality applicants. Today, UnLtd India funds fifty to seventy investees every year, together with its partner affiliates in Tamil Nadu, Hyderabad and Delhi

When quizzed about the challenges she has faced as a young woman entrepreneur in a male-dominated system, she replies, 'If being an entrepreneur is tough, then being a woman entrepreneur is tougher, and being a young woman entrepreneur is tougher still.' She recalls how in the early days, most questions and conversations at meetings were directed to Richard while she had to make double the effort to convince them of her competency. The situation was even worse in legal offices where they would not even look at her, and direct all questions to her male colleagues, even though she would be the one answering them. Her 'pet peeve', as she calls it, is men coming up to her in business meetings or conferences, and complimenting her on her physical appearance. While she has, by now, learnt to take biases in her stride, there have been incidents that still clearly rankle. Like the one where a man walked up to her when she was nominated for the Young Global Leader award in 2013 to tell her that her name must have been included for the sake of having a brown female on the list. She could not help retorting: 'Maybe the award had come my way because I deserved it.'

Never one to take things lightly, each incident has set her thinking about how she can contribute towards making a change in women's lives. On her agenda is to build a focused portfolio of 100 women-led-ventures within the next three years. Not only does she think that these women will become role models for their communities, but also they will tend to hire more women and bring about enduring change.

With so much on her plate, how does work–life balance work for her, I want to know. She admits unabashedly that it is the trickiest aspect of entrepreneurship as there is a real danger of turning workaholic—'founder's guilt', she reminds me, is a reality. With marriage on the cards in the next few months, she says resolutely, 'On my deathbed, I don't just want to be known for the work I did but also for the love for my family.'

For a person who has never let money be the driving force behind any important action or decision, the parameters of success lie way beyond a bloated bank balance and an expensive lifestyle. Success to her means not having any regrets in the winter of life. 'If at the age of seventy, I am able to count my what-ifs in one hand, I would count myself successful,' she quips. And that is also her advice to women sitting on the entrepreneurial fence: 'to minimize their regrets'. She recommends that they 'go with their instinct and take the plunge, for there never will be a perfect moment to do so'. Her word of caution is that while you can gain a lot from social entrepreneurship right from recognition to personal gratification, it demands a great deal of commitment, especially to the communities you are working with.

Above everything else is her belief in a larger power that ensured that so many things that she could not have planned, 'simply fell into place'. While this is a humbling thought, 'keeping it in your consciousness also helps to take the pressure off a little bit', she adds with a twinkle in her eye.

Pooja counts herself immeasurably blessed each time someone walks up to her to tell her that she has played a role in their success. Given the calling she has chosen for herself, this must happen every so often, I am sure!

WORDS OF WISDOM

- 'Money has no permanence, it ebbs and flows. Attachment to it is pointless.'
- 'Determining what you do not want to do is as important as discovering what you want to.'
- 'The more rejections we got, the more determined we became.'
- 'While there is a lot you can gain (from social entrepreneurship)—right from national and international recognition to personal gratification—it also demands a great deal of commitment, especially to the communities you are working with.'
- 'If being an entrepreneur is tough, then being a woman entrepreneur is tougher, and being a young woman entrepreneur is tougher still.'
- 'If at the age of seventy, I am able to count my what-ifs in one hand, I would count myself successful.'
- 'UnLtd India was simply meant to be. I am only a tool. While this is a humbling thought all right, keeping it in your consciousness also helps to take the pressure off a little bit.'
- 'Go with [your] instinct and take the plunge, for there never will be a perfect moment to do so.'

Snapshot

Birth sign: Virgo

Biggest role model: All our investees

Proudest moment: So many . . . all of them related to our investee's achievements

Oft-repeated quote: 'When you want something the entire universe conspires with you to achieve it.'

Favourite downtime activity: Dancing and travelling

Most inspiring author: Haruki Murakami

Three must-haves for aspiring female entrepreneurs:

- Unwavering belief in one's vision.
- Circle of mentors and supporters.
- Initial proof of need and demand from your customers and beneficiaries.

YUKTI KAPOOR MEHANDIRATTA

Entrepreneur, model and anchor

Founder:	Concept Exhibitions
Past corporate avatar:	Citibank and Barclays
Education:	Alumna of JDBIMS
Honours and awards:	Gladrags Mrs India Second Runner-Up, 2008
Just when you thought you had heard it all:	Host of Gladrags 2010 and *Science Show* on Topper TV

KEEPER OF HER OWN CONSCIENCE

A corporate banking job and oodles of good looks that helped her win the Gladrags Mrs India second runner-up title! That's more than what many of us can ask for. Not Yukti. Following her heart, she gave up a high-paying corporate job to set up Concept Exhibitions, an organization focusing exclusively on experiential learning for children to bring back the joy of learning through discovery. Next on her bucket list is to expand the scope of Concept Exhibitions to include special children and not die 'printing money'. All this while donning multiple hats of being an anchor and a model! That, in a nutshell, is Yukti Kapoor Mehandiratta for you.

'Change the way you look at things and the things you look at change'—Wayne W. Dyer, philosopher,
author, motivational speaker

A meeting with Yukti isn't a meeting you can forget in a hurry. First things first, she's a natural head-turner. But even before you start to paint her with the broad-brush strokes typically associated with a fashion model, you witness a highly intelligent and perceptive mind in action. In times when self-absorption has risen to a fine art, she believes, 'There is a larger purpose to life than to die just printing money.' You cannot help but sit up and take notice of this gutsy woman who has clearly taken a path less trodden.

The eldest of three daughters, Yukti, grew up in a close-knit family where each one of them looked out for the other. It fell upon young Yukti to take charge at home while her parents were away at work. Some of her earliest childhood memories are of standing up on a stool to be able to reach the gas stove to warm up lunch for herself and her siblings. Shouldering responsibilities at such a young age made her far more mature than most kids her age and she found herself easily included in all adult conversations.

With her natural good looks, her growing-up years in New Delhi saw offers for modelling come virtually knocking at her door. She reminisces how she could not take them up actively, as her father, in particular, did not look favourably upon modelling as a profession. There is a look of wistfulness on her face as she recounts, 'When getting ready for an early-morning shoot, I literally froze in my tracks to see my father's swollen eyes that spoke volumes of the sleepless night he had spent.' While any other youngster would be too starry-eyed with the glamour of the profession to harbour any second thoughts, young Yukti decided that it was not 'worth putting my parents through so much grief', and just like that, bid her modelling career adieu. It is another matter that destiny did have modelling plans in store for her later in life.

Joining a large bank immediately after a master's in mathematics heralded the start of a promising career. The bank also gave her more—it was here that she met her future husband. While Yukti saw him as her best friend and confidant, it was left to him to take the relationship to the next level. A task that he rose up to, going as far as to becoming a regular visitor to her home and endearing himself to her parents, no mean feat given their conservative outlook. His persistence finally won over her inhibition, and marriage ensued. He has turned out to be the perfect anchor for her dreams, supporting her every bit of the way, even if it means putting his own career on the line. She recalls how when she received an extremely attractive job offer in Mumbai, he had no qualms about giving up his job to accompany her and look for opportunities there.

Quizzing her on how modelling found a place in her life again amidst a demanding career, I am told that it was at her husband's insistence that she ended up applying for the Gladrags Mrs India contest when he chanced upon the form in an in-flight magazine. All she did was enclose some casual photographs that she already had, and the next thing she knew she was among the top ten finalists.

There is no mistaking the twinkle in her eye as she shares memories about the one-month residential workshop that all the contestants had to undergo before being brought on stage for the finale. 'Our batch of twenty-two final contestants of Gladrags Mrs India was unique in a lot of ways. It was amazing how we all instantly connected,' she reminisces. So much so that when the media wanted to do a 'behind the scenes' gossip segment, they were utterly disappointed to see the contestants speak well of each other. She breaks out into a mischievous laugh as she recalls how the segment could not be aired as they were told that they had been given the 'wrong' content.

Being declared the second runner-up is an experience she will always cherish, not so much for the victory but more because 'it challenged my own abilities and strength in different ways'. 'While the glory of winning the pageant remained with me for a year, the friendship I earned will remain with me forever,' she adds.

When queried if the idea of taking up modelling as a full-time career crossed her mind, she says in a matter-of-fact manner that the practical realities of being a married woman in an industry heavily biased in favour of the single and unattached, were not lost on her. Moreover, she confesses that she enjoyed the highs that came from applying her intellect as a banker too much to switch to modelling as a full-fledged career. There is no mistaking the amusement in her voice as she admits that unlike her, it took a lot of time for her colleagues and especially her boss to digest the fact that she preferred the role of a staid banker over that of a fashion model!

With a banking career on the fast track to success and a dream marriage, life was running smoothly till motherhood beckoned and the harsh reality of being a woman in the corporate world hit hard. The hurt is still there in her voice as she recounts how while discussing her maternity leave with her boss she was made to realize that her performance ratings and designation were likely to go down due to absence from work. Back to work after delivering twins, true to the boss's word, she was not only assigned a low rating but also given charge of an entirely new business to develop, with no formal training or support. 'It was as if I was being prepared for failure', she says, 'and I was determined to prove them wrong.' Instead of letting the enormity of the task daunt her, by dint of sheer hard work, she managed to develop an entirely uncharted territory, besides proving her naysayers wrong. Vindication for her efforts came the day her boss, in front of all her peers, revised her performance rating upwards and declared her an asset to the organization. The going, she admits, in those days was anything but easy—waking up early to nurse her children and then rushing to report to work on time, only to rush back home in the evening to nurse them again. The taunts at the office about her leaving work every day at 6 p.m. were unsavoury to say the least and even today it riles her that men can waste precious office time having their cigarette breaks but when women choose to work diligently through the day and leave work on time, they are heckled. And when we are talking of a drop-dead gorgeous woman like Yukti, there were other challenges too. The conversation turns sombre as she is reminded of how her colleagues used to dismiss her professional success as stemming from good looks. It pains her even now to think about how she was forced to 'downplay her looks' so that her colleagues would get past the stereotype and give her credence for her work.

The constant need to prove herself only because she was a woman, however, had somewhere begun to wear her down. There was also this growing desire within her to do something that served a purpose greater than just making money. During one brainstorming session with a friend on possible opportunities, she hit upon the idea of Concept Exhibitions, aimed at organizing experiential exhibitions where children can have fun while discovering new concepts. She recalls how the idea compelled her enough to finally hand in her resignation from her six-figure banking job.

As I ask her whether fear had any place at this stage, she candidly admits that 'there were indeed jitters and butterflies as I came from a salaried background. Used to a large salary hitting my account every month, the situation looked scary on the face of it, but somehow my core remained untouched and peaceful'. You get a glimpse of the steel beneath the beautiful exterior as she adds that even amidst this fear she had this firm belief that 'if you are true to your work, money will eventually follow. I think these are the times in life which help you realize how passionate you are about what you do.'

Other than the financial pressure, she reminisces about how there was no dearth of naysayers to add to the overall tumult in her life. Most people were quick to point to her extreme foolishness in giving up a high-paying job to pursue a nebulous goal. 'The definition of success is very clichéd in our minds,' she says wisely. 'If you are making money, you are successful; if not, you are labelled a failure. Don't all of us keep looking out of the corner of our eye to see if the other person is making more money or driving a better car or living in a bigger house? That's all there is to life for most of us'.

Societal pressure also came in the form of condemnation when as a new parent she was accused of neglecting her parental duties in pursuing her entrepreneurial dreams. She admits that the pressures were enough for self-doubt to set in. It was on one such occasion when she was being pulled in different directions that she sat herself down and asked an incisive question: 'Is there a need to prove my love for my children or my family on a daily basis. In that instance I got my own answers'. It was a moment of truth for her. 'It is only when people see your conviction that they start lending their support, but if you break down under pressure, they lose no time in breaking you further.' Having rid herself of the constant need to prove her commitment, she realized she was left with much more freedom and energy to focus on her goals. 'I think women need to shrug off the unnecessary burden of proving themselves as a good mother, wife and daughter-in-law all the time because if we exercise the passion we have within us for our dreams, then that passion will automatically and authentically flow in all our close relationships as well,' she says.

As for her work, the biggest challenge staring her in the face was to promote her events on a shoestring budget. She fondly recalls that among a host of detractors, her path also crossed some people who went out of their way to help her. Notable among them was RJ Anita of 94.3 FM who thought enough about her concept to mention it on her radio show and send a lot of footfalls to the exhibition.

Amidst all these challenges, her first Kids' Mela held at the World Trade Center turned out to be a roaring success; the three-day exhibition was the first of its kind to screen original curated children's films made in India, in partnership with the Children's Film Society of India (CFSI). The stupendous success of the exhibition paved the way for many more such events like the one organized in collaboration with the CFSI. Again a runaway success, Kids' Carnival, revolving around the concept of Swachhta and organized along with National Children's Film Festival held as part of Children's Day celebration, was graced by personalities such as Arun Jaitley and Sania Mirza. Next on Yukti's agenda is to take Kids' Mela to schools with autistic children as well as schools with spastic and HIV-infected students.

The journey, she admits, has not been easy. In the initial phase, she was forced to dig into her savings, which seemed substantial at the time of quitting her corporate job, but quickly eroded. The lowest phase for her came when she had to reach out to her parents briefly for financial support, something she had not done all her working life. But even during these tough times, there was the conviction that her future plans as an entrepreneur would not be dictated by money considerations. A strong believer in the power of intentions, her faith is evident when she declares that if you wish for something strongly enough, the whole universe conspires to make it happen for you.

Today, along with her entrepreneurial projects, she also keeps her other interests alive, namely modelling and anchoring. A natural at anchoring, her repertoire includes corporate shows, award ceremonies and TV shows, including hosting the Gladrags show in 2010. Going back to that stage was 'a homecoming of sorts', she explains. Only, instead of her own nerves, she now had to pacify those of the contestants. 'After all, I was a senior this time,' she quips good-humouredly. 'All I could tell them though was to enjoy the journey and leave everything in the hands of a bigger force.'

When asked what her advice to other budding entrepreneurs would be, she says with unabated enthusiasm: 'There is only one life, and the best way to live it is to listen to your heart. You just need to gather the courage to take that one baby step, and God will take ten steps for you.' For wannabe entrepreneurs, her advice is: 'Jump towards the side where the heart lies and the rest will be magical!'

Yukti has witnessed fame, money and glamour, but is strangely untouched by it all. Choosing a life of substance over a fat bank balance takes more than an ordinary drive and that is what makes Yukti's life truly remarkable.

WORDS OF WISDOM

- 'There is a larger purpose to life than to die just printing money.'
- 'If one is true to one's work, money will eventually follow.'
- 'I think women need to shrug off the unnecessary burden of proving themselves as a good mother, wife and daughter-in-law all the time because if we exercise the passion we have within us for our dreams, then that passion will automatically and authentically flow in all our close relationships as well.'
- 'There is only one life, and the best way to live it is to listen to your heart.'
- 'You just need to gather the courage to take that one baby step, and God will take ten steps for you.'
- 'Jump towards the side where the heart lies and the rest will be magical!'

Snapshot

Birth sign: Cancer

Biggest role model: A.P.J. Abdul Kalam, Shereen Bhan, Prasad Karmarkar

Proudest moment: Giving birth to my twins and, of course, when I delivered my first event successfully—Kids' Mela.

Oft-repeated quote: 'I can and I do.'

Favourite downtime activity: Playing with my twins

Most inspiring book/author: *The Secret* by Rhonda Bryan

One big dream for tomorrow: To have multiple intellectual properties under my company's umbrella and bring international recognition for each one of them.

Three must-haves for aspiring female entrepreneurs: Courage, commitment and clarity

ANISHA SINGH

Entrepreneur
Co-founder and CEO, Coupon Provider, Mydala

Co-founder and CEO:	Mydala, India's largest coupon provider
Past corporate avatar:	Centra Software, Boston
Education:	Alumna of American University, USA
Honours and Awards:	Recipient of Leading Woman in Retail Award, 2012 and

	Women Leadership Award at the World Women Leadership Congress, 2014
Just when you thought you had heard it all:	Yoga instructor Professional cake decorator

QUEEN OF (UN)AVERAGES

When Anisha Singh tells you, 'You cannot align your chips,' she isn't just spewing a cliché. Here is a woman who started out in life with a firm resolve of never running a business. For, as a youngster, she had seen her dad's business struggle. So, when it was time to build her career, she chose the stability of a corporate job in the land of opportunities. And yet, to the surprise and dismay of many, she not only moved back to India in a couple of years but also co-founded a company that had a very humble beginning. Today, this self-proclaimed 'Queen of Averages' is every start-up's role model, as her venture, Mydala, is valued at over Rs 1000 crore. This is her story of grit and gumption.

'If you can dream it, you can do it'—Walt Disney, cartoonist, animator

Having read a description of Anisha as 'Hurricane Anisha' who 'zips through her days with enough energy to put Hurricane Sandy to shame', on Mydala's website, I thought I was suitably prepared for my meeting with her. And yet, nothing can really ready you for meeting this powerhouse of energy and confidence. The Okhla office of Mydala was both an ideal setting and a fitting prelude to this meeting.

For someone who grew up with a strong resolve of becoming anything but an entrepreneur, Anisha's story is the stuff that dreams are made of. She co-founded Mydala, India's largest coupon company, with Arjun Basu (her long-standing friend and now her husband) and Ashish Bhatnagar. The company is today the poster organization of the dotcom space, having turned profitable at a time when many others are either continuing to burn cash or have shut shop.

'I was the queen of averages for the first part of my life,' she says, as we start to trace her childhood journey. That sounds discordant in the current setting, with Mydala being any start-up's dream. She continues to narrate how for the first fifteen to seventeen years of her life, she went about her ways without any goal. Two things she knew for sure though. The first, she didn't want to become a dentist. Her mom was a dentist and her tryst with injections and blood left the daughter unimpressed.

The second, she would NEVER take to business. With Mydala's phenomenal success, 'never say never' has become a standing joke in Anisha's life. As you probe her on this decision, she has a tale that endears young Anisha to you instantly. Her father, who was an ex-serviceman and involved in a thriving business with his father, started a real estate business of his own following a family tiff. While they continued to live in their family home and everything seemed fine, financially they fell upon hard times, so much so that paying even the school fee turned into a monthly challenge. She explains now she has this aversion to potatoes because that's what she ate as a child for the longest time, being one of the cheapest vegetables available. Back then, she knew for sure, that as an adult, she was going to pick up a stable job with a steady pay cheque and that entrepreneurship would not feature in her scheme of things. The solemn tone of the discussion suddenly perks up as you get a glimpse of Anisha's never-say-die attitude through an anecdote she narrates. A strong believer in the power of dreams, she recalls how even in that low phase, she never stopped dreaming. Every morning while on her way to the Air Force School, when her school bus passed by the sprawling houses of Palam Marg in New Delhi, she peered at them, confident that one day she would be a proud owner of one of them and not just a mere passer-by. This, at a time when owning just about any house was a luxury that they couldn't afford. She tells me how she doesn't let a single occasion go by when she does not tell her dad that the power of her dreams has today put him at his current Palam Marg address.

Not one to mince words, she admits that she was just an average student and even recalls how a professor during her undergraduate course held her up as a model for other students not to emulate, as he thought she wouldn't go far. A prediction that couldn't be further away from the truth!

Interning with the Discovery Channel post her undergraduate studies, she happened to meet someone who had studied political communication, and decided to follow suit. Accepted by the American University, USA became the setting for Anisha's sojourn for the next few years. She recalls how even there she remained quite uninspired early on, until a chance encounter with a teacher-turned-mentor egged her on to utilize her full potential. Armed with a new-found belief in herself, Anisha enrolled for an MBA programme. The high point came when she interned with the Olympus Group in the DC area led by a woman called Julie Holdren. 'Julie walked on water,' says Anisha. A mother to twins, she ran a start-up of 400 people and did thirty push-ups a day; Anisha knew that she wanted to be like her someday!

She confesses that the seeds of entrepreneurship were possibly sown even earlier when as a student, she babysat for $14 an hour. There's pride on her face as she recalls how she did that to support herself. The real taste of entrepreneurship, however, came about during her stint at Capitol Hill where she worked with the Clinton administration for National Women's Business Association. Merely twenty-one, she helped raise funds for innovative women-led businesses. She spent her weekends looking at thousands of business plans. The high point that made her look forward to her weekends, however, was that every plan came with a two-page note about a woman and her life. Anisha realized early that the world is 'full of some phenomenal women'.

As for her own career, she was still steeped in the concept of job stability and started to work for a large software firm in Boston, where she helped set up e-learning ecosystems for Fortune 500 companies. It was during this time that she saw a big market for e-learning solutions which she felt she could tap on her own. This was also a time when although she was perfectly comfortable with her life in New York, returning to India was a tape that had slowly but surely started playing in her head.

While she had enough experience of the domain, given her corporate stint in the area, taking the plunge was indeed a big decision, more so for someone who had grown up counting the merits of a steady income. Setting up a company meant deploying her hard-earned savings and redeeming her stock options towards an unchartered territory. Her own demons made the journey even tougher. Arguably, moving back to India was in itself a big decision and there were many cynics in the land of opportunity, who advised her against it. She was not only changing career midstream, but also her whole way of life with a change in country. When asked how she traversed this part of the journey, she recalls how she returned to India with only one suitcase in order to test the waters. Determined to leave nothing to chance, she particularly remembers meeting Deep Kalra of MakeMyTrip to get an industry perspective. Encouraged by his response, the one-suitcase visit to India turned into a permanent one. She recalls how consumed she was by the idea and its execution that she could not even go back to the US to shift her stuff. It was her sister-in-law who did all the spadework for the relocation.

With an eye on the growing e-learning market, KINIS Software Solutions was launched in 2007, as a joint venture company with a US-based firm. What started as a home-grown company soon started to provide high-end e-learning solutions to companies in the US and the UK and also to the domestic market. When asked if the journey was hunky-dory all along, she is quick to recall a stage early on where she was 'lying curled up on her couch' worried about the fact that she did not know how she would pay the next month's salary to her employees. Fortune as they say, favours the brave. That very month, the company got a large project that not only took care of the salaries but also put her comfortably on the road. 'As an entrepreneur,' she says her biggest learning has been that, 'you cannot always align your chips. You could be the richest person and life could still change in a minute.'

With KINIS software in self-sustaining mode two years later and a junior partner running day-to-day operations, Anisha began to explore new horizons. Researching online on various business models, she chanced upon a model in China where people got together physically, as a group, to avail of deals. Groupon at this time had only come into existence in New York, though far from a full-blown deal site that it is today. The idea resonated with Anisha in the Indian context especially, as Indians' love for a good deal is well known.

When asked if fear had any place, since this time, she was treading on an unknown path, she tells you how 'life literally happens'. While entrepreneurship wasn't a part of her broad plan in the first place, when opportunities came around she 'didn't overthink'. There's only one thing that she recommends, which is absolutely non-negotiable—'sufficient groundwork'. The one piece of advice that she has for wannabe entrepreneurs is to have a viable business plan and not just strive for a high valuation.

Beyond this, when considering entrepreneurship as an option, she says the only thing that helps is to think of the worst-case scenario. 'As long as you are sure of a roof over your head and food on your table, you cannot go too wrong.' A learning that clearly draws on her childhood experience. 'After all, if you fail once, you can always start over again,' she says determinedly.

Mydala, she explains, had a very humble beginning; its first office shared space with her mother's dental clinic. Soon after the company came into existence, Anisha also found out that she was carrying her first child. She is at her witty best in describing a spate of interviews where a pregnant woman sat next to a dental chair and explained to candidates the 'big picture' of how Mydala is set to break new ground. If people bought in to her vision, it, of course, speaks of her sheer passion and belief but also, as she is quick to point out, 'it takes some serious commitment' on the part of the candidates to come on board a new venture. On her part, she made sure that she recruited such committed people. Most of her core team, she proudly mentions, has stayed on to see the journey of Mydala, no mean feat in today's scenario of growing attrition.

The pregnant interviewer went on to work into the wee hours of the morning every day, surviving on 'daal naan in true start-up culture', so much so that everyone started telling her that Daal Naan is what she should name her progeny. She recalls how even on the night of her delivery, she was in the office till 1.30 a.m. With characteristic wit, she tells you how there was 'no time for post-partum depression' and she was back to work in exactly ten days, losing the twenty-eight kilograms put on during her pregnancy pretty quickly.

You cannot but appreciate the resilience of this woman as she goes on to explain how on the business front there was a time when Mydala had its due diligence done and as much as closed in on a term sheet with an investor. Only that, on the day of the formal document-signing, the investor backed out. While it was a devastating blow to the business, it did teach her some very important lessons, the primary being the 'need to innovate'. While the company went on to be funded by Info Edge later, the lessons learnt stand the test of time. Irrespective of the cash in the bank, she confesses to run an extremely cash-conscious operation, so much so that 'it takes some thinking to buy something as small as plants for the office'.

Did she have a brush with the patriarchal face of the start-up world? Anisha tells me how during the initial fundraising stage, she was discounted by many an investor, one even calling her 'too pregnant'. While she laughs it off now with a shrug, the irony is only too apparent. She recalls how the investor chose to speak to her male co-founder referring to her only in the third person, confident that after childbirth, 'she wouldn't come back'. A conversation that Anisha chose to end by telling the investor in no unequivocal terms: 'It is my company and the end call will be mine.' She is quick to point out though that for every such person, she has also met some really 'cool people' who have turned out to be her mentors.

More than the glass ceiling, Anisha feels it is the ability to second-guess their own capabilities that are stopping women in achieving their true potential. That, and the fact that as a gender, women aren't too supportive of each other. She points out how women make 'great friends, super sisters, mothers and daughters' but somehow, 'we don't stand up as much for fellow women professionals'. That explains why after informally mentoring women, Anisha is now toying with an idea to do it formally. As she says, 'People who have a voice need to give back to society.'

As the conversation veers to her own work–life balance, Anisha points out that it indeed is a tough call for spouses sharing a workspace. When asked if she would recommend spouses to come together to co-found a company, she quips, 'This needs not just second-guessing but perhaps guessing yourself forty times.' She cautions that it takes a toll on the work–life balance as office talk finds its way home. Besides, 'It takes a seriously secure guy to report to his wife. But they do it secretly at home anyway!' As for the working-mom guilt, Anisha confesses her brush with it is as frequent as brushing her teeth. Spending quality time with her kids is therefore uncompromisable. 'Between 7 p.m. and 9 p.m. [the time earmarked for her daughters], you need to be God to get my attention,' she says determinedly. Such single-minded devotion was sure to be rewarded and Anisha's reward came when, at her daughter's latest parent–teacher meeting, she was told how her daughter seems to have been brought up with so much genuine love and effort that it shows in her demeanour. Anisha recalls bawling unabashedly in front of the teacher and other parents.

When queried about her future plans, she promises to 'ring the NASDAQ bell someday'. It is a business goal all right, she tells me, but more than that she wants her daughter to grow up with enough role models. 'It is only when our daughters hear of more women entrepreneurs will they think it's the norm rather than the exception,' she says. Sure enough, her daughter wants to grow up to run her own company!

'With all its ups and downs and your own initial fears, has the entrepreneurial journey been worth it and would you recommend it to others?' I ask. Anisha's answer puts a stop to any further conjecture. 'I have woken up each day with gratitude, charged and excited. How many people get to do it?' Perhaps this is the most incisive question in the journey of entrepreneurship and in the journey of this book!

WORDS OF WISDOM

- 'As an entrepreneur you cannot align your chips. Life cannot be aligned.'
- 'As long as you are sure of a roof over your head and food on your table, you cannot go too wrong.'
- 'You could be the richest person, and life could still change in a minute.'
- 'Have a viable business plan. Don't just strive for a high valuation.'
- 'People who have a voice need to give back to society.'
- 'Between 7 p.m. and 9 p.m. [which is her time with her daughters] you really have to be God to get my attention.'
- 'We don't stand up as much for fellow women professionals.'
- 'It is only when our daughters hear of more women entrepreneurs will they think it's the norm rather than the exception.'
- 'I have woken up each day with gratitude, charged and excited. How many people get to do it?'

Snapshot

Birth sign: Pisces

Biggest role model: Anyone who has fought odds and accomplished something in life

Proudest moment: Yet to come!

Oft-repeated quote: 'Ask yourself what would I do if I weren't afraid? And then go do it!'

Favourite downtime activity: Catching up with family and friends over sushi and wine

Most inspiring books/authors: Maya Angelou, Malcolm Gladwell, Sheryl Sandberg's *Lean In*. Love the fact that many new authors are writing books featuring inspiring female protagonists!

One big dream for tomorrow: To ring the NASDAQ bell

Three must-haves for aspiring female entrepreneurs: Perseverance, belief in oneself, a strong support network

DARE TO BE CONVERSATIONS

Let us continue the 'Dare to Be Conversations' by building a community of women entrepreneurs in order to learn from each other's experiences. If you are one of those who have Dared to Be, or know someone who has or want to be inspired by reading about many more such accounts, please join the community at www.facebook.com/Daretobeconversations.

It is by sharing our collective experiences and beliefs that we can outshout that persistent naysaying voices in our heads.

Till then, *Dare to Be*!

ACKNOWLEDGEMENTS

I am thankful to the many people with whose support I could 'Dare to Be' and so could this book.

My deepest thanks go out to the fourteen wonderful women who have been featured in this book. Not only did you give us your time, but also a piece of your heart in telling your personal stories. In the journey of the book, inspiration was one thing we were never short of. I hope we have been able to do justice to your hugely motivating stories and that many other women benefit from the story of your lives. From starting out as subjects of the book, so many of you became friends for life.

A warm thank you is due to Kanishka Gupta, our agent and a dream merchant. You could certainly set new records of proactivity, as I heard from you within minutes of writing to you with the concept of the book. Everything else followed in record time and thus began the journey of this book.

Thanks are due to the entire team at Penguin Random House for believing in the concept of the book. Thank you, Milee Ashwarya, for your unstinting support. Finding someone who believed so strongly in the power of these stories, as I did, in Gurveen Chadha, has been extremely empowering, to say the least.

This book wouldn't have been written but for Puja Singhal, my childhood friend and co-author. Our numerous brainstorming sessions on each chapter remain the high point of writing this book.

And finally, I want to thank a few people who haven't just contributed to this book but also to everything that I am today. Foremost among them are my parents, Vijay and Usha Paul, for believing in me wholeheartedly. But for you, I wouldn't be what I am. You taught me to believe that the only thing one is limited by is one's own vision. Thanks are also due to my sister, Dipti, and her angel, Ahaan, for lighting up our lives.

Thank you, Suhaani, my darling daughter, for braving through those times when you needed me and I needed to write.

I am truly indebted to my husband, Sachin Sachdeva, for his unstinting belief in me. You goaded me on to put fingers to the keypad; without your faith, this book would have only remained a fond retirement dream.

Last but certainly not least, a warm thank you to my extended family, in-laws and friends, who, on numerous occasions, reached out to me to tell me that my writings had touched them at some level. All of you, in some measure, are responsible for this daring act.

Rinku Paul

A journey of a thousand miles begins with a single step and sometimes the journey can turn out to be as rewarding as the final stop. So it has been with writing this book. While the book may have started out as a labour of love, triggered more out of our desire to bring to the fore issues plaguing women in business and as entrepreneurs, it has ended up infusing me with a greater sense of self-belief and a renewed sense of optimism. The opportunity to meet and listen to the life stories of the fourteen amazing women featured in this book has truly been the highlight of this endeavour. I cannot thank them enough for trusting us with their life stories, as well as for their unwavering patience, encouragement and support.

A big thank you goes to Kanishka for making the path to publishing so much easier for us. Your swift response and quick advice has always been much appreciated.

Thank you, Penguin Random House, especially Gurveen, for making it possible for many to draw inspiration from the life stories of these amazing women.

To my mother I will remain ever grateful for passing on her love for the written word, and to my father for always being there whenever I have needed him.

My husband and kids remain my greatest inspiration. They remain my biggest critics as well as my staunchest cheerleaders, forever egging me on to take up new challenges.

I reserve my biggest thanks for you, Rinku, for simply put, this book would not have been possible without you.

Puja Singhal

A NOTE ON THE AUTHORS

Rinku Paul

A corporate career spanning over sixteen years with the news channel Aaj Tak, a part of the India Today Group, made up the first part of Rinku's career. Till she decided to pursue her dream—impacting people's lives!

She is now an internationally certified life coach, corporate trainer and neurolinguistic programming practitioner. In co-founding a writing studio, The Muse, she has also given her first love, writing, a professional outlet.

Rinku holds an honours degree in English, followed by an MBA in marketing.

She lives in New Delhi with her husband and her daughter.

Puja Singhal

With more than a decade spent in corporate life, strategizing how best to marry business and people as an HR specialist, Puja decided to call it quits to plunge into the world of content writing. She is now a full-time writer and the co-founder of the writing studio, The Muse.

Puja holds an honours degree in political science and an MBA in human resource management.